# The Bottom Line

# The Bottom Line

## Determining and Communicating the Value of the Special Library

Joseph R. Matthews

2002
Libraries Unlimited
A Division of Greenwood Publishing Group, Inc.
Westport, Connecticut

Libraries Unlimited
A Division of Greenwood Publishing Group, Inc.
88 Post Road West
Westport, CT 06881
1-800-225-5800
**www.lu.com**

ISBN 1-59158-004-8

P

In order to keep this title in print and available to the academic community, this edition was produced using digital reprint technology in a relatively short print run. This would not have been attainable using traditional methods. Although the cover has been changed from its original appearance, the text remains the same and all materials and methods used still conform to the highest book-making standards.

Smart people are not those that remember every detail of everything but those that know where to look for knowledge.

—Tim McEachern and Bob O'Keefe

# Contents

# Acknowledgments

It is rare for an author to write a book without the contributions of a number of people. Therefore, I would like to acknowledge the comments and suggestions of several people who have made this book better. Suzanna Krebsbach, corporate librarian for Santee Cooper, which is located in Moncks Corner, South Carolina, Sharyn J. Ladner, Assistant University Librarian at the University of Miami, who has been involved in the Special Libraries Association for a number of years; and Kathy Wright, librarian for SPAWAR, U.S. Navy located in San Diego, California. All three reviewed the draft manuscript and made a number of substantive suggestions that helped provide additional clarity. Susan DiMattia, former president of the Special Libraries Association, and Olga Wise, corporate librarian at Compaq, also provided helpful comments. Any errors or lack of clarity in the information presented in this book are obviously my responsibility, not theirs.

I am also indebted to the many libraries that provided photocopies and loaned me books so that I might better understand the topic of assessing the value of special libraries through that wonderful library service called interlibrary loan.

All types of libraries, but especially special libraries, are indebted to the contributions of Donald W. King and Jose Marie Griffiths. They have dedicated a significant portion of their careers to studying, understanding, and writing about the contributions and value of a library. Their enthusiasm and willingness to share the knowledge they have gained through conference presentations, seminars, articles, books, and personal conversations are appreciated by many, including this writer.

I also would like to acknowledge the staff at Libraries Unlimited for their helpful assistance in producing this book, especially Martin Dillon for his helpful comments on the first draft; Sharon DeJohn for her insightful copyediting; and Edward Kurdyla for his encouragement to complete this project.

Joe Matthews
Carlsbad, CA

# Introduction

*Where is the wisdom we have lost in knowledge?*
*Where is the knowledge we have lost in information?*
—T. S. Eliot

What is the most effective way for a library director to convey to management the value of the library to the larger organization? In times of economic uncertainty, special librarians are being asked to justify the existence of the library or run the risk that resources will be reduced or eliminated altogether.

Librarians are involved in the daily provision of a variety of information services. They are committed to the belief that information is an essential tool for any organization. Most librarians have personal, anecdotal evidence of the experience of users who have benefited from having information readily and reliably available. The problem is that this evidence is uncertain at best and clearly not quantifiable. Thus it cannot provide a basis for evaluating the overall effects of the value of providing library services. However, a structured approach can provide librarians with the necessary information so that they can demonstrate a positive return on investment (ROI) for the library.

Special libraries have a number of characteristics that should be acknowledged prior to a discussion of evaluation of the library and its services. Among these are the following:

- The library collection is typically small but highly specialized in subject matter.

- Clients are typically only staff of the larger organization, and their interests are known and can be explained fairly accurately.

- The library is part of a larger organization, such as a private corporation, nonprofit organization, trade organization, or government agency, that shares and supports the mission of that organization.

- There is a tradition of being very responsive to the clients of the library, often articulated as providing high-quality or timely service.

Special libraries include libraries in corporations, law firms, hospitals and other medical facilities, research organizations, accounting firms, consulting organizations, and government agencies. Yet even for a similar size and type of library, the resources available for research and library services vary due to factors such as tradition, external economics, and political decision-making procedures within the organization.

Many company managers view the library as an overhead expense that can be safely cut in the face of an economic downturn. And although many special librarians are well versed in business and management practices, other librarians have difficulty evaluating services from an organizational perspective. The typical evaluation methodologies used by librarians to evaluate library services are different from those used by their managers. Librarians are trained to apply techniques that measure efficiency but tend to be less comfortable with cost analysis, staff productivity measures, or assessment of benefits. Yet it is from the broad perspective (reflected in these latter measures) that senior managers expect to evaluate library services, as well as other services in their organization. Thus, there is a seemingly insurmountable chasm separating professional librarians from their managers when it comes to assessing the utility of a library.

Often senior managers intuitively understand and recognize the importance of the services library and information centers provide. At the same time, these managers are frustrated in their inability to link current library activities, products, and services with direct benefits for the organization. A 1990 survey of senior managers in large U.S. corporations revealed that more than 60 percent could not give a specific

> *If you don't keep score,*
> *you're only practicing.*
> **—Vince Lombardi**

value of the library in their organization.[1] Were this same survey conducted again today, it is likely that similar results would emerge. These same managers also indicated that there is little managerial consensus on how a library adds value or how value should be measured. In some cases, senior managers may have known of the value of "their" library but, seeing the library as a possible competitive asset, would likely be hesitant to reveal this information and thus consider it to be privileged or confidential.

## EVALUATION EFFORTS

The library and information services profession has a considerable body of literature relating to the measurement of performance. The American Library Association (ALA) and other professional associations have developed a variety of "input measures" and created general library standards based on these measures.[2] In the late 1980s and 1990s, ALA developed a new set of initiatives focused on output measures.[3] The Special Libraries Association, due in part to its long-standing interest in assisting librarians to identify the value of special libraries, has published a number of works on this topic,[4] including the following:

- *President's Task Force on the Value of the Information Professional* (1987)
- *President's Task Force on the Value of the Information Professional: An Update, Highlights and Conclusion* (1990)
- *Valuing Corporate Libraries: A Survey of Senior Managers* (1991)
- *The Impact of the Special Library on Corporate Decision-Making* (1993)
- *Special Libraries: Increasing the Information Edge* (1993)
- *The Value of Corporate Libraries* (1995)
- *Valuing Special Libraries and Information Services* (1999)
- *Valuing Information Intangibles* (2000)

Yet despite these efforts some confusion persists. What performance measures should a library employ? Should a library focus on input measures, process measures, or output measures? Should some combination of measures be used? How does benchmarking relate to performance measures? How do managers determine the outcomes of a library? Does a library need to hire a consultant to measure actual impacts or outcomes of library services? Given a plethora of techniques that can be employed to try to assess outcomes, how does one choose?

# TOP MANAGEMENT EXPECTATIONS

What then is the management team of any organization expecting when they consider the value of a library or information center? The management team of any organization would like to be able to assess the quality of and value of the library, the information technology department, the human resources department, or any other "support" department in basically the same way. Is it possible to establish in clear, measurable ways the contribution of the department to the overall success of the organization? The manager responsible for the library, not the library director, may choose several criteria to evaluate the performance of the library:

- **Money.** What is the library budget, and how is it used? How does the library save money for the organization, and how much does it save?

- **Time.** How much time does the library save the employees of the organization, thus increasing productivity?

- **Value-added information.** What information does the library produce that cannot be obtained elsewhere? Is raw information organized and synthesized into digestible formats?

- **Prevention of litigation.** Does the library provide information that prevents legal problems for the organization?

- **Timeliness of information.** Is information provided in a timely manner? Does it help employees meet deadlines?

- **Relevance of information**. Is the information provided helpful to the library's users? Are the librarians knowledgeable in the subject areas of the organization?

- **Amount of information**. Is the appropriate amount of information retrieved for each customer?

- **Accuracy of information**. Is the information provided accurate?

- **Proactivity**. Does library staff go the "extra mile" to get information when it is a priority? Does the library anticipate the information needs of its users?

- **Consistent service**. Is the level of service consistent day-to-day? Does it vary by who is at a service point?

- **Error-free service**. Are information and service provided in the preferred format and by the required deadline?

- **Friendliness**. Does library staff seem to care about customers? Would users want to come back to the library?

- **Professional business image**. Do library staff members look and act like professionals? How well does the library fit into the organization's culture?[5]

The problem with such an approach is that the criteria selected by a manager may or may not be "in tune" with the services of the library or the information needs of the organization. At times, the manager may have an implicit or explicit agenda for the evaluation to justify a planned course of action.

# INFORMATION ENVIRONMENT

The modern information milieu is rich and diverse in resources, but it is precisely the richness that often overwhelms people. How do people cope with a hundred or more e-mails per day (the "carbon" copy and e-mail distribution lists, which do little to improve the productivity of an organization)? One study found that 71 percent of white-collar workers felt stressed by the amount of information that they received each day and 60 percent felt overwhelmed.[6] How does one cope with a flood of industry journals?

Performing a search using an Internet-based search engine can be a very frustrating experience. (Which of the 1,500 + sites that are retrieved as a result of a search should one examine?) Even in this electronic age the use of paper within an organization continues to increase. People are bombarded with calls from a telemarketing industry that continues to grow. David Shenk calls this information glut a thickening *"data smog."*[7] Herbert Simon, the Nobel prize-winning economist, observed that, "What information consumes is rather obvious: it consumes the attention of its recipients. Hence, a wealth of information creates a poverty of attention."[8]

Richard Saul Wurman has suggested that the ever-widening gap between what we understand and what we think we should understand creates "*information anxiety*."[9] It is the black hole between data and knowledge, and it happens when information doesn't tell us what we want or need to know. Thomas Davenport and John Beck feel that the new currency of business is the attention that we pay to information and information-rich messages.[10]

Economics is concerned about scarce resources. Given the phrase "information economy," the focus would seem to be information as a scarce resource, yet according to Richard Lanham, "We are drowning in information, not suffering a dearth of it. Dealing with this superabundant flow is sometimes compared to drinking from a fire hose. In such a society, the scarcest commodity turns out to be not information but the human attention needed to cope with it."[11]

> *What people really intend when they speak of information is meaning, not facts. Undoubtedly we're bombarded with too many facts—isolated bits of data without a context. . . . To assign meaning always requires more information to organize what we already have. . . . More meaning and fewer facts. That's the idea, anyway.*
> **—Michael Crichton**[12]

Rosenberger's Laws of Information[13]

1. Faster information drives out slower information.

2. Inexpensive information drives out expensive information.

3. Directly delivered information drives out information not directly delivered to the customer.

4. Content-rich information drives out content-lean information.

5. Customized information drives out mass-produced information.

6. Timely information drives out untimely information.

7. User-friendly information drives out less user-friendly information.

8. Secure, stable information drives out less secure, less stable information.

# TERMINOLOGY

The terms "user," "reader," "client," "customer," and "patron," although they have some slight differences in meaning, are assumed to refer to the same person who seeks and receives information from a library or information center. One survey found that "patron" was the term of preference for librarians from all types of libraries.[14] In the special library setting, it is assumed that a majority of libraries identify these individuals as "clients" or "customers" as a not-so-subtle reminder that the library and all of its resources are there to serve the needs of the parent organization.

# NOTES

1. James M. Matarazzo and Laurence Prusak. Valuing Corporate Libraries: A Senior Management Survey. *Special Libraries*, 81 (2), Spring 1990, 102–10.

2. Vernon E. Palmour, Marcia C. Bellassai, and Nancy V. DeWaite. *A Planning Process for Public Libraries*. Chicago: American Library Association, 1980.

3. Douglas Zweizig and Eleanore Jo Rodger. *Output Measures for Public Libraries: A Manual of Standardized Procedures*. Chicago: American Library Association, 1982; Nancy Van House, Mary Jo Lynch, Charles McClure, Douglas Zweizig, and Eleanore Jo Rodger. *Output Measures for Public Libraries*. Chicago: American Library Association, 1987; Charles McClure, Amy Owen, Douglas Zweizig, Mary Jo Lynch, and Nancy Van House. *Planning and Role Setting for Public Libraries*. Chicago: American Library Association, 1987; Thomas A. Childers and Nancy A. Van House. *What's Good: Describing Your Public Library's Effectiveness*. Chicago: American Library Association, 1993; Nancy Van House, Beth T. Weil, and Charles McClure. *Measuring Academic Library Performance: A Practical Approach*. Chicago: American Library Association, 1990.

4. *President's Task Force on the Value of the Information Professional*. Washington, DC: Special Libraries Association, 1987; *President's Task Force on the Value of the Information Professional: An Update, Highlights and Conclusion*. Washington, DC: Special Libraries Association, 1990; James M. Matarazzo, Laurence Pusak, and Michael R. Gauthier. *Valuing Corporate Libraries: A Survey of Senior Managers*. Washington, DC: Special Libraries Association, 1991; Joanne G. Marshall. *The Impact of the Special Library on Corporate Decision-Making*. Washington, DC: Special Libraries Association, 1993; Jose-Marie Griffith and Donald W. King. *Special Libraries: Increasing the Information Edge*. Washington, DC: Special Libraries Association, 1993; James Matarazzo and Laurence Prusak. *The Value of Corporate Libraries: Findings from a 1995 Survey of Senior Management*. Washington, DC: Special Libraries Association, 1995; *Valuing Special Libraries and Information Services*. Washington, DC: Special Libraries Association, 1999; Frank H. Portugal. *Valuing Information Intangibles: Measuring the Bottom Line Contribution of Librarians and Information Professionals*. Washington, DC: Special Libraries Association, 2000.

5. Holly J. Muir. *Conducting a Preliminary Benchmarking Analysis: A Librarian's Guide.* Universal City, TX: Library Benchmarking International, 1993.

6. Institute for the Future. *Workplace Communications in the 21st Century Workplace.* Menlo Park, CA: Institute for the Future, May 1998.

7. David Shenk. *Data Smog: Surviving the Information Glut.* San Francisco: HarperEdge, 1997.

8. Herbert Simon. Designing Organizations for an Information-Rich World, in Donald M. Lamberton (Ed.). *The Economics of Communication and Information.* Cheltonham, UK: Edward Elgar, 1997.

9. Richard Saul Wurman. *Information Anxiety.* San Francisco: Doubleday, 1989.

10. Thomas H. Davenport and John C. Beck. *The Attention Economy: Understanding the New Currency of Business.* Boston: Harvard Business School Press, 2001.

11. Richard A. Lanham. *The Electronic Word: Democracy, Technology and the Arts.* Chicago: University of Chicago Press, 1993, 227.

12. Michael Crichton. *Electronic Life: How to Think About Computers.* New York: Random House, 1983.

13. Joseph L. Rosenberger. Answers Are Easy. *Across the Board*, April 1997. Reprinted with permission.

14. John H. Sandy. By Any Other Name, They're Still Our Customers. *American Libraries*, August 1997, 143–45.

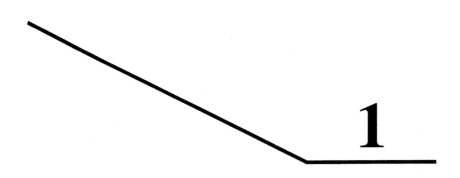

# How Libraries Add Value

*That which today calls itself science gives us more and more information, an indigestible glut of information, and less and less understanding.*

—Edward Abbey

Data, whether numeric or textual, become information when they are organized and imbued with purpose or intelligence resulting from the assembly, analysis, or summary of data into a meaningful form.[1] The intent of information is, after all, to "inform." Another way to define "information" is in the form of an equation:

$$data + context = information.$$

Information is the outcome when relationships among data are established. Instituting the structure, relations, rules, and conditions used to establish those relations among data elements is what distinguishes really good information. As noted by Daniel Bell and Nicholas Negroponte, information is increasingly replacing matter and energy as the primary resource of society; in other words, the economy is moving from atoms to bits.[2]

> **Data are the "unorganized sludge" of the Information Age.**
>
> **—Robert Lucky[3]**

It is important to distinguish between two concepts: the information content of a message and the service or resources used to provide or transmit the message.[4] Information is the content of the message, or that which informs. Information resources are the services, the packages, and the support technologies and systems used to generate, store, organize, manipulate, and provide access to these *information-bearing entities* or what Arlene Taylor calls "information packages."[5]

Robert Taylor, a professor at Syracuse University, has spent a good part of his career focusing on the processes that add value.[6] As shown in Figure 1.1, the process of transforming data into information and then knowledge so that it is suitable for decision making involves a series of value-added activities. A library is involved with three principal processes: organizing processes, analyzing processes, and judgmental processes.

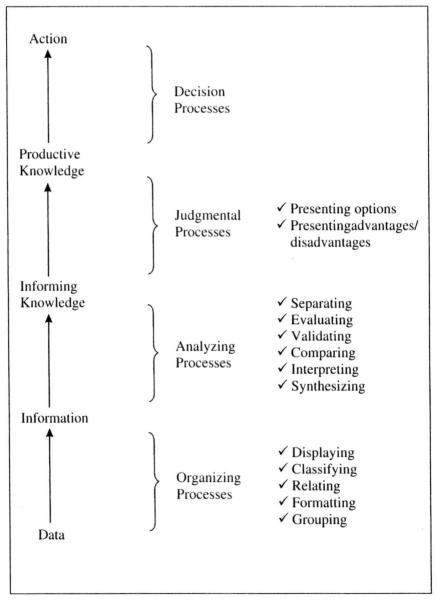

Figure 1.1. Value-Added Spectrum

# VALUE

One of the major difficulties with the concept of "value" is that it has many facets or dimensions, which suggests that care should be exercised when the term "value" is used. Consider the phrases "positive value," "negative value," "dollar value," "exchange value," "monetary value," "apparent value," "use value," and "esteem value," to name but a few of the ways in which "value" is used in everyday conversation. This problem of defining value is compounded when it is applied to information. Information has attributes that are unique when compared to other resources.

All evaluation efforts start with the hypothesis that the user of information gives value to the specific information when the information is used. The information must first have an expected value-in-use to arouse the interest of the user. The user then decides to use the information or not. The value of information can be identified if the role of information can be traced to a specific work task and the output of the task.

It is also important to note the unique characteristics of information as a commodity. Most economic goods display such properties as appropriateness, divisibility, scarcity, and decreasing returns from use. Information differs from these typical properties in that

1. It is not easily divisible;

2. It is not inherently scarce (although it can be perishable)—many people can own the same information and not deprive others;

3. It does not exhibit decreasing returns to use but can increase in value the more it is used;

4. It is self-regenerative or feeds upon itself;[7] and

5. It is costly to produce but cheap to reproduce. There are no natural capacity limits for additional copies.[8]

In a study completed for the Council on Library Resources, Tefko Saracevic and Paul Kantor examined the concept of value in philosophy and economics as part of their development of a *Derived Taxonomy of Value in Using Library and Information Services*.[10] They identified four types of philosophical value:

- **Intrinsic value**. Being worthy or good in and of itself. For example, good health.

*What the customer buys and considers value is never a product. It is always ... what a product or service does for him.*

**—Peter Drucker**[9]

- **Extrinsic or instrumental value.** Contributes to something that is intrinsically valuable. For example, eating in moderation contributes to good health.

- **Inherent value.** An experience, contemplation, or understanding that contributes to intrinsic value. For example, viewing the Grand Canyon would lead to a good experience.

- **Contributory value.** Contributes to the value of the whole. For example, using shampoo when showering.

Given the constraints of trying to apply the philosophical approach—for example, it is difficult to demonstrate the intrinsic value of being informed—Saracevic and Kantor turned to the field of economics as one holding more promise.

The pragmatic approach taken by economists, who hold that value is the worth of something that contributes to wealth, has yielded better results. Adam Smith's distinction between "value-in-exchange" and "value-in-use" is one of the foundational principles of economics and has been used to assist in determining the value of information.

The value-in-exchange theory is most easily understood in terms of price. People exchange money for products. The price paid is the accepted indicator of the products' value. The concept of "exchange value" not only includes the agreed-upon price between two parties but also the time and effort an individual is willing to invest to receive the perceived benefits. Attempting to use this approach to identify the value of a library and information services is difficult because real money is not exchanged.

To overcome the limitations of exchange or price theories of value, economists developed a second set of theories called value-in-use. Analysis using value-in-use or "utility theory" focuses more specifically on wants, usefulness, satisfaction, demands, and so forth. Clearly the meaning of an information "package" is related to its value. Value-in-use means that the benefits of the information to the user define its meaning. Further, value is separated from the container or means of conveying the information. It would seem to be appropriate to separate use of information and the effect of use.[11]

Using the value-in-use approach, the value of information can be divided into three categories:

- **Normative value approach.** This approach relies on rigorous, formal models that use uncertainties (assessing risk) in relation to decision making. Restrictions are placed on the types of information considered and thus this approach has little value for measuring a library and its information services.

- **Realistic value approach.** This approach attempts to measure the before and after consequences of information or an information service on the performance of decision makers. The realistic value approach has been used by a number of individuals in the valuation of library and information services.[12]

- **Perceived value approach**. This approach assumes that users can recognize the value of information (or the benefits gained/lost). This methodology assumes that clients can assign a monetary value or indicate a ranking if a scale is used. Saracevic and Kantor used this approach when they developed their *Derived Taxonomy of Value in Using Library and Information Services*. Their taxonomy is discussed in Chapter 7.

## ADDING VALUE

To understand how value can be added to information, it is important to understand the information-seeking process, which is illustrated in Figure 1.2. The client is an individual who is seeking or receives information from a library or information service. Robert Taylor suggests that a client has several possible criteria for judging the usefulness of a service, and these are shown in summary form in Table 1.1. Each of the user criteria is discussed in greater detail in the following sections.

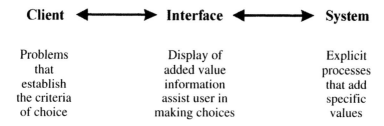

| Client | Interface | System |
|---|---|---|
| Problems that establish the criteria of choice | Display of added value information assist user in making choices | Explicit processes that add specific values |

**Figure 1.2. Information-Seeking Process**

## Table 1.1. User Criteria for Assessing Value

| User Criteria | Interface (Value Added) | System (Examples of Value-Added Processes) |
|---|---|---|
| Ease of use | Browsing | Alphabetizing |
| | Formatting | Highlighting |
| | Mediation interface | Linking |
| | Orientation interface | |
| | Ordering (sorting) | |
| | Physical accessibility | |
| Noise reduction | Access (item identification) | Indexing |
| | Access (subject description) | Vocabulary control |
| | Access (subject summary) | Filtering |
| | Linkage | Linking |
| | Precision | |
| | Selectivity | |
| Quality | Accuracy | Quality control |
| | Comprehensiveness | Editing |
| | Currency | Updating |
| | Reliability | Analyzing and comparing data |
| | Validity | |
| Adaptability | Closeness to problem | Provision of data manipulation capabilities |
| | Flexibility | Relevance output ranking |
| | Simplicity | |
| | Stimulatory | |
| Time savings | Response speed | Reduction of processing speed |
| Cost savings | Cost savings | Lower costs |

*Source:* **Adapted from Robert S. Taylor.** *Value-Added Processes in Information Systems.* **Norwood, NJ: Ablex, 1986, 50. Reprinted by permission.**

# Ease of Use

Ease of use elements reduce the difficulty in using a system. The amount of effort required by the client to use a system or information service will determine whether the system or service is used. This observation has been formalized as "Mooers' Law," which states: "An information retrieval system will tend not to be used whenever it is more painful and troublesome for a customer to have information than for him not to have it!"[13] From the perspective of the system interface, several things might be done to assist the client.

*Browsing* allows the client to scan an information environment just as browsing a physical collection of materials in a library allows the client to see what is physically close to a title (determine what is in the neighborhood). One of the consequences of classification systems in libraries is that they facilitate browsing. Browsing, sometimes called scanning, is particularly helpful when the information seeker is not clear as to the scope or boundary of a problem or of the relationships between various groups of data and information. Browsing, not surprisingly, facilitates serendipity. Harvey Neville states in his First Law of Serendipity: "In order to find anything one must be looking for something."[14]

*Formatting* is the arrangement of data/information in ways that allow for more efficient browsing and assimilation. From the system's perspective it might mean having the capability of displaying information in a variety of predetermined formats. As systems move to personalization, one of the implications is that they will support the user's preferences (whether the format is predefined or not). In a text environment, formatting may mean use of labels for each field of data, use of different fonts or font sizes, or highlighting to make the process of browsing faster. The presentation may also include the use of nontextual elements such as graphs, images, sound, or video, and use of visualization software to recreate a phenomenon in nature, for example, the formation of a tornado.

*Mediation interface* is the means used to assist an information-seeking individual in getting answers. Such means may range from providing user assistance in the form of reference services to the use of cross-references in a catalog or index. Another example of mediation interface is a librarian providing a search intermediary service.

An *orientation interface* is the assistance provided to help clients use a particular information source or service themselves, for example, learning to use an index or directory found in print or an online database. In some libraries, a formal program of orientation is usually called *bibliographic instruction* or *information literacy*. The orientation interface is focused on systems but may involve a librarian providing one-on-one assistance to a client.

*Ordering* is focused on the process of organizing a body of materials. A majority of librarians would almost automatically assume that the ordering process means use of a classification system. However, Richard Wurman has pointed out that there are five ways to organize information: category (classification), time, location, alphabet, and continuum.[15] Several of these methods might be used at the same time, for example, use of a classification system and then alphabetizing within a category.

*Physical accessibility* is concerned with the ease of access to information contained in a physical space. (Given the time that has elapsed since Taylor developed these categories, and the importance of desktop delivery of information as an important service for special libraries, perhaps this category should be called *virtual accessibility* rather than physical accessibility.) A number of studies, especially in the public library setting, have demonstrated that there is a direct correlation between the convenience of physical access (as expressed in the distance, time, and energy it takes to visit a library) and use of the library. Similar experiences have been noted in the special library environment.[16]

## Noise Reduction

Noise reduction involves a series of activities that will withhold or exclude information, include appropriate information, and improve the precision of the information retrieval process.

*Access (item identification)* provides to a user the location or identification of an item or record through the use of a systematic physical description. In bibliographic systems, the citation provides a means of access. A library information system uses a richer, often MARC-based, bibliographic cataloging record as the means of identification.

*Access (subject description)* provides additional access points through the use of additional indexes using precoordinated subject headings, subject terms, and other descriptive approaches. The value of adding subject descriptors in the cataloging process is that it brings together similar items in a collection that have been randomly dispersed by each author's arbitrary choice of words used in a title.

*Access (subject summary)* provides a summary of the content of an item. The idea of the summary is to capture the essence of the work with fewer words. The summary may take the form of an executive summary, an abstract, the table of contents, the book jacket summary, and so forth. Research has shown that adding content to a MARC bibliographic record in the form of a summary will improve the user's information retrieval experience.[17]

*Linkage* provides links and pointers to items and other resources, whether in a library's collection or located externally, that will expand the user's information options. The links may take several forms:

- An indexing system, as in the form of cross-references.

- Works or a series of books about a particular broad topic, for example, nuclear medicine.

- A thesaurus structure that provides access to the relationships among and between terms (broader than, related terms, and narrower than).

- Other forms of the same work, for example, an image of the original document (the Declaration of Independence), a sound or video recording of someone reading the document, and so forth.

- Hypertext linking capabilities afforded by the Web browser.

- A "pathfinder," which indicates a variety of resources that the user might wish to consult about a particular topic.

- Access to a directory of individuals who are knowledgeable about a particular topic within the organization.

*Precision* is the capability within an information retrieval system to select only relevant documents (records) and reject irrelevant ones in response to a request to the system. (It is the number of retrieved relevant items divided by the total number of items retrieved.) Precision is contrasted with *recall*, which is the ability to retrieve as many relevant records or documents as possible. (Recall is the number of retrieved relevant items divided by the total number of relevant items.) For example, consider a collection of documents that has 100 relevant titles in the collection. Should the search retrieve 85 documents (60 of which are relevant and 25 not relevant), it has a recall of 60 percent (60 out of 100) and a precision of 70 percent (60 out of 85).

There is a wide body of research about precision and recall that suggests that as precision is increased, recall declines.[18] The performance of most library online catalogs and many Internet search engines will vary greatly, but it is not uncommon to see systems operating at around 50 percent recall and 50 percent precision.

*Selectivity* is focused at the input point of a system based on assumptions of the appropriateness of certain groups or classes of information using the characteristics of a specific individual or group as a starting point. In some ways, selectivity is analogous to the personalization capabilities that most people have experienced if they have shopped using the Internet. Using information about the past experiences of the user, including what items have been purchased, the system can recommend items or records that are likely to be of interest. A bibliographic information retrieval system might ask the user to choose a definition for a word as a way to reduce the noise in the retrieval process. (The user might choose the definition for a bridge in a musical string instrument, thus allowing the system to eliminate the 20 + other definitions for the word *bridge* from the retrieval process.)

## Quality

From the user's perspective, the issue of quality actually involves several value- added processes that deal with the accuracy, comprehensiveness, and reliability of information.

*Accuracy* reflects the system's capabilities that ensure that the information entering the automated system is error-free. In other words, the system provides a number of consistency checks to ensure the accuracy of the data entered into a system. These consistency checks might be as simple as verifying the length of a field of data, or ensuring that the data are only numeric, have a certain structure, and so forth. The consistency checks might be more complex and, for example, employ a series of rules or "if-then" statements to ensure that a complete record adheres to a specific standard.

*Comprehensiveness* is focused on how complete the coverage is for a particular discipline or subject area (for example, physics). Knowing that a particular information resource is thorough makes that resource one with high added value.

*Currency* is the added value process that ensures that a database reflects the latest information; that is, how frequently are records added or updated?[19] The publisher of a journal printed twice a month could make online access timelier by posting articles scheduled to appear in the next print issue on a weekly basis.

Currency is also reflected in the capabilities of a system to redirect a user's request to other, more appropriate terminology. The fact that in most disciplines the vocabulary is constantly evolving means that if an authority control system is used, the user will more likely find everything on a particular topic, regardless of the vocabulary used in the search request. Thus, an authority control system that is updated on a regular basis and adds cross-references will improve the currency and value of the database.

*Reliability* is the added value process that provides the assurance that an information system or service is consistent over time and thus allows the user to develop a sense of trust. The user is able to judge the consistency of the system or service through prolonged use, and this results in an intangible, yet very important, value as a reliable, trusted source of information.

*Validity* is a system process that indicates to the user that the information that has been presented is sound. The system might signal to the user with notes that there may be problems with the research design, the manner in which data were collected, an indication of the source of funding for the research (which might disclose a bias), and so forth.

## Adaptability

Adaptability is concerned with system and interface attributes that assist the user in finding appropriate information in non-subject terms. The focus here is on a specific user-defined problem.

*Closeness to the problem* is dealt with by tools that improve adaptability, including the capabilities of a system, typically reflected in the user interface that assists the user who has a specific information need and will help in solving a definite problem. This may be a specific user interface to solve a particular problem; it may be context-sensitive help, customizing the display of information so that it is controlled by the user; and so forth.

*Flexibility* provides to the user a variety of tools to dynamically, in real-time, change how the information is displayed. The information might be sorted in several ways or displayed using a variety of graphical formats. A system is also flexible if the user can accomplish the same result using a variety of means: instructing the system using commands, clicking on an icon in a tool bar, choosing an option in a pull-down menu, and so forth.

*Simplicity* describes those value-added processes that assist in making the meaning or content of information found in a record or group of records easier to understand. The user interface, if it is well designed, will result in clarity and a lack of ambiguity when information is displayed. This might involve the use of data field labels that are clear in their meaning and do not contain library or technology jargon (for example, how many users would know what "main entry" means?). How many of us have received an error message or viewed online instructions to accomplish a task and been totally befuddled, even after reading the message or instructions several times?

*Stimulatory* value-added processes are designed to explain the unfamiliar and perform useful services for the parent organization. This might involve hosting sack lunches, at which guest speakers from within the organization explain their latest research or project. In the online arena, this might mean using software collaboration tools, participating in a videoconference, and so forth.

## Time Savings

Library and information centers are designed primarily to be of value to the user by saving the user's time. Time savings are achieved using two particular tools. First is the library's collection. Knowing the likely information needs of the users of the special library, the professional staff creates and maintains a collection of information resources that are likely to be of value to the user. Rather than attempting to find the desired item by themselves, the user visits (physically or electronically) the library to obtain the required information package. Second, the library provides access to a variety of online databases. Although users can in most cases use these electronic resources directly, they will often turn to a trained intermediary to conduct the search to save time and improve the search results.

Given the importance of time savings to most organizations because time savings have a direct correlation to improved productivity, libraries may wish to examine the speed with which their various information services are currently provided. For the last few years, the business and technology press has been discussing changing the way an organization conducts its business to compete with existing and start-up companies that are able to develop and deliver new products and services in a more timely manner. Often this shortening of the new product and services development cycle is referred to as "Internet time."

The variety of information resources is essentially infinite, yet the demand for information is limited by the number of working hours in a day. How the library assists customers in becoming more productive is the key driver of how they will focus their attention on the tasks they need to accomplish. One effective way to accomplish this is to simplify the information into a form that is preferred by the customer.[20]

## Cost Savings

Cost savings, not surprisingly, are the actual savings that are achieved as a result of using the library or information service. The focus here is on actual dollar savings, and although in a number of cases the user will be unable to even guess as to the value of receiving a specific document or piece of information, in other cases the user can give a fairly precise estimate of the cost savings that will result.

> *The act of arranging information becomes an act of insight.*
> **—Edward Tufte**[21]

# SUMMARY

A library or information center will use a number of value-added processes in day-to-day activities. Among the value added tasks or activities are

Selection and acquisition;

Serials control/claiming;

Creation of abstracts or enhanced bibliographic records;

Selective dissemination of information;

Providing access to online resources;

Providing reference services;

Timely document delivery service;

Outsourcing activities; and

Evaluating and recommending online resources.

In most settings, libraries are considered to be a "good thing." The problem for most libraries is that few of their transactions are monetized. Hence, users or funding decision makers have little understanding of the costs of operating a library and may not know the value of the library.

One of the clear implications of this discussion on the value-added processes within a library or information center is determining what information services are of the most value to the individuals who use the library and to the parent organization itself. This important issue is addressed in the following chapters.

# NOTES

1. J. McGee and Laurence Prusak. *Managing Information Strategically.* The Ernst & Young Information Management Series. New York: John Wiley, 1993; R. Walker, Ed. *AGI Standards Committee GIS Dictionary.* London: Association for Geographical Information, 1993.

2. Daniel Bell. *The Coming Post-Industrial Society.* New York: Basic Books, 1973; Nicholas Negroponte. *Being Digital.* New York: Alfred A. Knopf, 1995.

3. Robert Lucky. *Silicon Dreams: Information, Man, and Machine.* New York: St. Martin's Press, 1989.

4. Y. M. Braunstein. Costs and Benefits of Library Information: The User Point of View. *Library Trends,* 28, 1979, 79–87; and Fritz Machlup. Uses, Value, and Benefits of Information. *Knowledge: Creation, Diffusion, Utilization,* 1, 1979, 62–81.

5. Arlene Taylor. *The Organization of Information.* Englewood, CO: Libraries Unlimited, 1999.

6. Robert S. Taylor. *Value-Added Processes in Information Systems.* Norwood, NJ: Ablex, 1986.

7. George P. Huber. The Nature and Design of Post-Industrial Organizations. *Management Science,* 30 (8), 1986, 928–51.

8. Carl Shapiro and Hal R. Varian. *Information Rules: A Strategic Guide to the Network Economy.* Boston: Harvard Business School Press, 1999.

9. Peter Drucker. *The Essential Drucker.* New York: HarperBusiness, 2001.

10. Tefko Saracevic and Paul B. Kantor. Studying the Value of Library and Information Services. Part I. Establishing a Theoretical Framework. *The Journal of the American Society for Information Science,* 48 (6), June 1997, 527–42; and Tefko Saracevic and Paul B. Kantor. Studying the Value of Library and Information Services. Part II. Methodology and Taxonomy. *The Journal of the American Society for Information Science,* 48 (6), June 1997, 543–563.

11. Fritz Machlup. Uses, Value, and Benefits of Information. *Knowledge: Creation, Diffusion, Utilization,* 1, 1979, 62–81.

12. M. M. Cummings. *The Economics of Research Libraries.* Washington, DC: Council on Library Resources, 1986; Aatto J. Repo. The Dual Approach to the Value of Information: An Appraisal of Use and Exchange Values. *Information Processing & Management,* 22 (5), 1986, 373–83; Michael E. D. Koenig. Information Services and Downstream Productivity. *Annual Review of Information Science and Technology,* 25, 1990, 55–86; M. Feeney and M. Grieves, Eds.. *The Value and Impact of Information.* London: Bowker Saur, 1994.

13. Calvin N. Mooers. Mooers' Law or, Why Some Retrieval Systems Are Used and Others Are Not. *American Documentation,* 11, 1960, 204.

14. Christine L. Borgman. *From Gutenberg to the Global Information Infrastructure: Access to Information in the Networked World*. Cambridge: MIT Press, 2000, 94.

15. Richard Saul Wurman. *Information Anxiety*. New York: Doubleday, 1989.

16. Jose-Marie Griffiths and Donald W. King. *Special Libraries: Increasing the Information Edge*. Washington, DC: Special Libraries Association, 1993, 101.

17. Pauline Atherton. *Books Are for Use: Final Report of the Subject Access Project to the Council on Library Resources*. Washington, DC: Council on Library Resources, 1978; E. Peis and J. C. Fernandez-Molina. Enrichment of Bibliographic Records of Online Catalogs through OCR and SGML Technology. *Information Technology and Libraries*, 17 (3), September 1998, 161–72.

18. Cyril Cleverdon defined precision and recall in the 1950s. See C. W. Cleverdon, J. Mills, and E. M. Keen. *Factors Determining the Performance of Indexing Systems*. London: Aslib Cranfield Research Project, 1966. A number of literature reviews have discussed the topic of relevance. See T. Saracevic. Relevance: A Review of and a Framework for the Thinking on the Notion in Information Science. *Journal of the American Society for Information Science*, 26, 1975, 321–43; L. Schamber. Relevance and Information Behavior. *Annual Review of Information Science and Technology*, 29, 1994, 3–48; and S. Mizzaro. Relevance: The Whole History. *Journal of the American Society for Information Science*, 48, 1997, 810–32. A more recent study examined the use of relevance by individuals in a virtual library setting. See Mary Ann Fitzgerald and Chad Galloway. Relevance Judging, Evaluation, and Decision Making in Virtual Libraries: A Descriptive Study. *Journal of the American Society for Information Science*, 52 (12), October 2001, 989–1010.

19. Time value of information, for example stock market price quotes for a particular stock, is examined in greater detail in Carl Shapiro and Hal R Varian. *Information Rules*. Boston: Harvard Business School Press, 1999.

20. Bill Jensen. *Simplicity: The New Competitive Advantage in a World of More, Better, Faster*. Cambridge, MA: Perseus Books, 2000.

21. Edward R. Tufte. *Visual Explanations: Images and Quantities, Evidence and Narrative*. Cheshire, CT: Graphics Press, 1997.

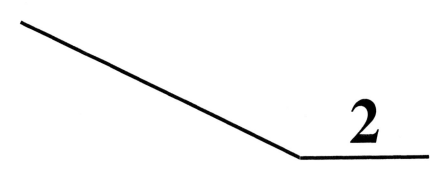

# 2

# Evaluation

*Insistently, persistently, relentlessly, the new manager musk ask, What for? What is it that we're in business for? What is this process for? This product? This task? This team? This job? What are we doing here anyway?*

—James Champy

Over the years the professional literature has produced an almost constant stream of articles reflecting on the need for quantitative and qualitative measures of libraries and their services. Rather than taking a broader perspective, these articles generally focus on a particular measure or group of measures. Often at the heart of these measures is an attempt on the part of a librarian to find some means or measure that will indicate the "goodness" of the library and its services.

Measures are a benchmark for many things. They can tell us *where we've been, where we are*, and *in what direction we are heading*. Intelligent use of measures can guide our decisions and assist us in making meaningful comparisons. The quality movement evolved from measurement-intensive disciplines, and measurement continues to hold an important place, for example, in such prestigious competitions as the Malcolm Baldrige National Quality Award.

Measurement relies on the collection and analysis of data, which are then compared to certain yardsticks, such as standards, goals, objectives, other similar libraries, and so forth. Peter Hernon and Ellen Altman suggest that there are at least eleven assessment questions that can be asked:

How many?

How economical?

How accurate?

How well?

How reliable?

How satisfied?

How much?

How prompt?

How timely?

How valuable?

How courteous?[1]

When a library is established, it is provided with a set of *resources*. Those resources are organized and directed so that they have the *capability* to provide a set of services. These capabilities are then utilized. Once utilized, the information that has been provided has the potential for a positive, beneficial *impact or effect* on the organization. The relationship among these variables is illustrated in Figure 2.1.

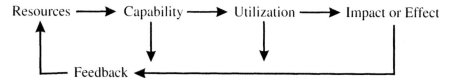

**Figure 2.1. General Evaluation Model. Adapted from R. H. Orr. Progress in Documentation—Measuring the Goodness of Library Services: A General Framework for Considering Quantitative Measures, in Donald W. King (Ed.). *Key Papers in the Design and Evaluation of Information Systems*. Westport, CT: Greenwood Press, 1978. Reprinted with permission.**

As shown in the generalized evaluation model, feedback can and often is employed by the library to make adjustments in other variables. For example, as service levels may decline as utilization increases, feedback can be used to make adjustments by increasing resources so that service levels are improved. The feedback is facilitated through the use of measures.

As shown in Figure 2.2, different types of measures are used to assess each of the four variables. The *input measures* are associated with the resources or inputs that have been allocated to the library. These input measures are also the easiest to quantify and gather. Librarians will often speak of their annual budget, number of professional staff, size of the collection, and so forth. All of these are examples of input measures of the resources provided by the larger organization.

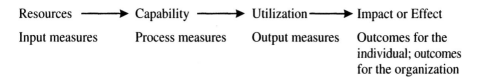

Figure 2.2. Evaluation Models and Their Associated Measures

*Process measures* are focused on the activities that transform resources into services offered by the library and as such are internally directed. Process measures are reflected in an analysis that will quantify the cost or time to perform a specific task or activity. For example, the cost to order an item, the cost to receive a journal title, and the time it takes from when a journal title is received until it is placed on the shelf for clients to use are all process measures. Process measures focus on a particular service or function within the library. They are ultimately about efficiency. Efficiency answers the question, "Are we doing *things* right?"

*Output measures* are used to indicate the degree to which the library and its services are being used. More often than not, output measures are simply counts to indicate volume of activity. For example, annual circulation, number of people entering the library, and number of reference questions answered are all output measures. Historically, use of output measures was regarded as a measure of goodness; after all, the library's collection and its services were being used, often intensively so! Therefore, the library was doing "good."

To fulfill their objectives most efficiently, most medium- to large-sized libraries are organized into two units, technical services and public services. Technical services transform the inputs into a form that is suitable for the library's clients. The public services arm of the library is concerned with providing a bridge between the available library resources and the client, and thus is focused principally on outputs.

*Outcomes* indicate the impact or effects of the library and its information services on the individual. The outcomes on the individuals then have a cumulative impact on the larger parent organization. Outcome measures are the most difficult to assess, and in a majority of cases reported in the literature have involved the use of a consultant and a major data collection effort to calculate the results. This area is complicated by the fact that some of the outcome measures are assessed directly, while in other cases indirect measures are used. To further complicate matters, the value being measured may be tangible or intangible.

Outcomes ultimately address the issue of effectiveness. Effectiveness answers the question, "Are we doing the *right* things?" Outcome measures center on the impact of the library on the parent organization; in other words, they have an outward focus as opposed to the inward focus of efficiency or process measures. One of the implications of focusing on process measures and outcome measures is that the library may lose sight of the "big picture" and concentrate on process improvements. Doing more things faster is no alternative to doing the *right* things.

All of these types of measures are addressed in greater detail in the following chapters.

# EVALUATION IMPLICATIONS

There are many reasons for evaluating a library or of one or more of its information services.[2] Among the objectives that may exist for an evaluation are the following:

- **Appropriateness of organizational goals or program objectives**. Evaluation for this reason is designed to assist the library in determining if its services are meeting the needs of its clients as well as addressing the broader issue of assessing the impact of the library on its larger or parent organization.

- **Objective accomplishment**. This approach focuses on the effectiveness of a library service and tries to assess the degree to which a specific objective has been reached. The results of the measurement activity can give occasion to celebrate real results that staff members can see and believe.

- **Appropriateness of resource allocation**. This approach assesses how efficient the library is in using the resources that have been provided to it. Such measures allow the library to know what it is doing right and what needs to be improved.

- **Monitoring and accountability**. This evaluation focuses on the assessment of existing library programs and services and as such usually uses process (efficiency) and output (effectiveness) measures. In some cases, the data collected are governed by an outside funding source.

- **Impact assessment**. This approach determines to what degree the service or program has "made a difference." The attempt here is to learn what impact or outcomes are the result of the service or program rather than how efficient the service provided is.

- **Assessment of an innovative program**. The assessment of a new program, by definition, will have little or no history to use as a backdrop to the evaluation effort. The evaluation will likely combine process (efficiency), output (effectiveness), and impact measures.

- **Fine-tuning of library services and activities**. The objective of this type of assessment is to periodically review how well the library is doing in providing a service, often a long-standing service. The primary focus is on the efficiency of the operation. You can't know if you are improving quality or performance without measuring results.

- **Program continuance or discontinuance**. The goal with this type of appraisal is to determine whether a service should continue to be provided or be discontinued. The data normally collected focus on effectiveness and the impact of the information service on its clients and the larger organization. If the service was discontinued, what alternatives exist for those individuals within the organization who need the service?

One problem facing any librarian is to recognize a possible reluctance to perform a program evaluation if that results in the elimination of a rarely used or costly program. Some librarians may be reluctant to eliminate those services that have run their course and are no longer needed or are of marginal value.

In addition, a library that embraces evaluation should recognize the following:

- Evaluation means that library staff members and the library's funding decision makers will be making value judgments about what the library *should* be doing, about *how cost-effectively* the library is operating, and what criteria might be used to assess the library's *effectiveness*.

- Evaluation should be preceded by a clear statement of goals and objectives.

- The fact that evaluation is being discussed and used means that change is both possible and desirable (a fact not always appreciated by library staff).

- Evaluation does require that some staff time and organizational resources be consumed as a part of the evaluation process.

## SUMMARY

This chapter demonstrates that an evaluation model provides perspective about the relationship among and between different types of performance measures. Having a better understanding about the different types of measures will allow librarians to more effectively choose the measures that will assist them in communicating the value of the library to their funding decision makers.

## NOTES

1. Peter Hernon and Ellen Altman. *Assessing Service Quality: Satisfying the Expectations of Library Customers*. Chicago: American Library Association, 1998.

2. Peter Hernon and Charles R. McClure. *Evaluation and Library Decision Making*. Norwood, NJ: Ablex Publishing, 1990.

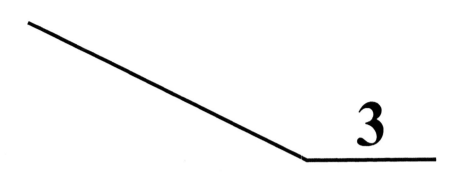

# Evaluation Techniques
# and Methods

*When you measure, you can understand,*
*when you understand, you can control,*
*when you control, you can improve,*
*when you improve, you can achieve your goal.*

—Edward Demming

This chapter reviews the variety of evaluation techniques that can be used to gather performance measures for a library and its information services. In addition, there is a brief summary of the various areas and services within a library.

## REASONS FOR EVALUATION

The collection and use of performance measures within any organization, including a library and its information services, may be done for a variety of reasons, including the following:

- **Comparison**. The library may wish to determine how efficient it is in performing a specific function or range of functions when compared to another library or a group of "similar" libraries. The evaluation data might also be compared to best practices in the profession or to the library's goals or objectives.

- **Diagnosis**. In some cases, measures may be used to determine whether a specific function or activity is being performed well or needs some management attention to correct a problem.

21

- **Information**. Performance measures may be gathered as a means to communicate the performance of the library or information center to the library's funding decision makers and stakeholders.

- **Justification**. Decision makers may gather process measures as a way to justify continuing an activity in-house as opposed to outsourcing it. As the volume of activity within the library increases, performance data can be used to justify the need for additional staff and other resources.

- **Orientation**. A variety of performance measures may be used as a means to provide an orientation to the library's decision makers, especially newly assigned decision makers, about the range of services provided by the library and the measures used to judge the value of the library.

- **Rewards**. Performance measures, in particular process measures, can be used to assess the improvements in an individual's or a unit's productivity. Based on these improvements, rewards (monetary and otherwise) can be distributed.

- **Sanctions**. Performance measures can also be used to impose penalties on an individual or unit if performance (quality, speed of service, volume of service, and so forth) declines.

# METHODOLOGIES

In general terms, an evaluation is more likely to use an objective approach as compared to a subjective methodology. An objective evaluation methodology gathers data and information, which are then analyzed and reported. A subjective evaluation methodology uses the experience and knowledge of the individual, be it a library manager or a consultant, to assess a library service. Although there are strengths and limitations to both approaches, generally the majority of evaluations will use the objective approach.

Similarly, evaluation methodologies can be divided into those that are obtrusive and unobtrusive. With the obtrusive approach, those participating in the evaluation are aware of the evaluator's presence, whether directly (e.g., via an oral interview) or indirectly (e.g., through a written survey). With an unobtrusive evaluation, the individuals being evaluated are unaware of the evaluator's presence. A majority of evaluation methodologies use the obtrusive process.

Measures in and of themselves have a number of observable characteristics. When considering a measure, check to see whether it has the following desirable features:

- It is objective and unbiased.

- It is inexpensive to collect data.

- It is an appropriate measure of the service or activity.

- It accurately reflects what is being measured.
- It is quantifiable.
- It can be uniformly interpreted.
- It is statistically reliable.

## Qualitative versus Quantitative Measurements

Quantitative measures are always expressed as numbers. A performance measure is composed of a number and a unit of measure. The number reflects the magnitude (how much) and the unit of measure provides meaning (what). The unit of measure might be presented as percents, degrees, fractions, counts, ratios, and so forth. Performance measures allow one to control an activity, and controlling an activity allows one to manage it. Quantitative measures are useful because

*If you can't measure it, you can't manage it.*

**—Peter Drucker**[1]

*If it moves, measure it! Otherwise paint it.*

**—Old Navy saying**

- They are very specific;
- They can be compared and the data can be tracked over time;
- Data in numerical form can be subjected to statistical analysis; and
- Numeric data help to eliminate bias.

Qualitative measures might be numeric, but their focus typically is on the quality of the work or activity being performed. Qualitative measures can be used to assess feeling, opinions, perceptions of quality, and so forth using a Likert scale.

## Specific Methodologies

There are a number of useful evaluation methodologies, discussed in the following sections.

### Surveys

The use of surveys is a time-tested evaluation methodology. The data to be gathered are carefully determined and the survey questionnaire is often pretested before the actual data collection process begins. The wording of questions typically is carefully considered because this can have a major impact on the validity and utility of the data and the analysis. Similarly, the way respondents can answer a question is also important; True/false, multiple choice, range of options (Likert scale—the ever-popular agree/disagree questions), and so forth force respondents to choose from alternative answers. Surveys can be self-administered or administered in person by the individual gathering the data. The latter option allows for follow-up and clarification questions.

Despite the inherent problems associated with designing and administering surveys, they remain a popular tool among librarians.[2] Surveys are often used to gather information about behaviors, attitudes, beliefs, and feelings. The results of the survey should be tabulated and summarized to reflect what has been learned. Some of the more frequently used surveys are a general library services satisfaction survey, assessment of a particular service, and a collection/document delivery fulfillment survey.

## Sampling

The data collection process may involve every individual who uses the library service, or a representative subset of individuals may be selected from the total group. This subset is called a sample. The purpose of a sample is to minimize the time, energy, and cost associated with the collection and analysis of data. One important consideration when sampling is to ensure that an adequate number of respondents participate (sample size) so that any statistical analysis will be valid (statistically significant) and the results will then be applicable to the entire population. Random sampling will generally allow the resulting statistics to be viewed as more representative of the group compared to a sample that is drawn during designated periods.

Sampling can be done with a population of clients (user surveys, satisfaction surveys), materials (examining a sample of the library's collection), and data (performing an analysis of a sample of circulation data, for example). Types of sampling include

- *Simple random sampling*—every item or individual has an equal chance of being included in the sample;

- *Stratified random sampling*—the total population is divided into groups and then a sample is selected from each group;

- *Systematic sampling*—the sample is chosen on the basis of a rule, for example, every nth item;

- *Quota sampling*—some portion of the sample is chosen based on a specific characteristic (demographic or other characteristic); and

- *Cluster sampling*—the population is divided into clusters and then a sample is drawn.[3]

## *Interviews*

The data being collected may be gathered using interviews. Generally, interviews will follow a script of questions, but an unstructured approach can be fruitful, especially when the researcher is just beginning to attempt to understand a situation or service.

When a group of individuals is interviewed at the same time, this process is usually called a focus group. A group needs to be small enough so that everyone can participate but large enough to provide a variety of perceptions—typically seven to ten people. When using a focus group, a facilitator guides the group in exploring the topic using some predefined questions. Follow-up clarifications may be needed to really understand what the group is saying. Another one or two staff members are there to observe and record comments of the participants. Focus group sessions are often audio- or videotaped.

## *Observation*

The individual gathering the data may observe an activity or service to understand the activities involved in a process or simply to gather information.

## *Case Studies*

A case study is a written report of a particular situation, for example, evaluating a library and its services using a variety of methodologies to determine what approach provides the greatest value. This approach is typically employed by an academic researcher and would not normally be done by a special librarian.

# EVALUATION MEASURES AND METHODS

As shown in Table 3.1 (page 26), the need or type of evaluation determines the particular evaluation measures used. Each of the measures has strengths and disadvantages, which are explored in greater detail in the next section.

A wide variety of measures can be used, depending on the focus of the evaluation. The major measures that are more frequently used are discussed here.

*Counts or tallies.* A count or tally is often used as an input measure, such as the number of volumes in the collection or size of the library (square feet), and also as an output measure to determine how frequently a service or facility is used. The count may be for a specific, limited period of time (for example, number of reference questions answered from 1:00 P.M. to 2:00 P.M.) or for a longer period of time (for example, a day or a week). The appeal of a count is that the data are easy to collect although there may be some variation in their accuracy; a staff member may neglect to tally a service when busy assisting the next client!

## Table 3.1. Types of Evaluation.

| Focus | What Is Measured? | Measures |
|---|---|---|
| Extent | Size | Counts, ratios, formulas (e.g., Clapp-Jordan Formula for Academic Libraries), Conspectus (Research Libraries Group, Academic Research Libraries, OCLC) |
| Efficiency | Cost | Ratios, weighted averages (HAPLR Index, benchmark comparisons |
| Quality | Intrinsic quality or goodness | List checking, citation analysis, impressionistic |
| Performance | Achievement of goals or objectives | Use, user satisfaction, availability |
| Effectiveness | Relationship between performance and efficiency | Cost-benefit analysis, other approaches |

*Ratios.* A ratio is used to indicate the relative size of something. It might be the proportion of the collection devoted to technical reports compared to the total collection, or the percentage of reference questions that take longer than 10 minutes to answer compared to all reference questions. Often time ratios are expressed as a percentage. Ratios are typically used to compare one library to another (percent of budget spent on acquisitions, percent of professional staffing per number of employees in the organization, and so forth).

*Formulas.* Formulas, as applied in the library field, are statements, especially an equation, of a rule or a relationship that exists between different factors. Researchers often develop mathematical formulas in an attempt to reduce a series of relationships, often complex, between various variables. For example, the Clapp-Jordan formula attempts to specify the minimum size of an academic library based on such factors as number of faculty and total number of students enrolled.[4] Formulas were also a part of a number of state library standards for public libraries.

*Questionnaires.* A questionnaire or survey might be distributed in-person, mailed, e-mailed, or linked to a Web site. Questionnaires can be designed to focus on a specific service or provide a broad-based perspective on the library and its information services.

*Weighted systems.* The appeal of a weighted system is that it will combine a number of measures and then assign a weight to one or more of the measures so that a particular one is emphasized more than others. Hennen's American Public Library Rating, or "HAPLR Index," is an example of a weighted system.[5]

*List checking.* An individual knowledgeable in a subject area or a committee created by a professional association will create a list of recommended holdings. The purpose of the list, for example a list of quality titles reflecting a minimum collection size, is to allow other libraries to see how their collections "measure up" (and consider purchasing the missing titles).

*Citation studies.* In a number of communities, for example, legal, medical, scientific and technical, and academic, information flows through "invisible networks" of colleagues and scholars with common interests, regardless of their location. Much of this communication is formally acknowledged as authors create journal articles, write reports, give speeches at conferences, and so forth. References, in the form of citations, are made in this communication process both to acknowledge sources of ideas and information and to provide further background for a reader. Studies that use citation indexes published by the Institute for Scientific Information and others allow a library to determine the extent to which the most frequently cited works are to be found in a library's collection of journals.

*Content analysis.* This approach uses a systematic analysis of the words, phrases, and concepts that a respondent provides to an open-ended question or document. This approach may use a computer program to provide an analysis, or the individual preparing the analysis can code (categorize) the words and phrases. This approach is fairly time-consuming.

*Think-aloud protocol.* This methodology asks respondents to verbalize their thought processes and opinions while interacting with a library resource to accomplish a particular task. The objective is to discover *how* a user performs a specific task and the problems that he or she encounters. This process is sometimes called a user protocol.

*Impressionistic.* A consultant may be asked to evaluate a specific library service, a portion or all of the library's collection, or the management and operation of the library itself. The resulting report will obviously reflect the person's impressions and observations rather than expressing some objective measures. Even though the expert's report might, for example, suggest a number of titles that should be found in the library's collection, this is still a subjective view of the library.

# EVALUATING SPECIFIC LIBRARY SERVICES

The rest of this chapter provides a summary of the tools typically used to evaluate specific library services, internal operations, the library's collection, and so forth. The remaining chapters of the book focus on the library as a whole, rather than a particular service.

Evaluating or measuring specific library services is an important topic that has generated a number of articles and books. These services are the library's collection, the online catalog, reference services, document delivery, technical services, and the library's facilities.

## Collection Evaluation

An evaluation of a collection will typically employ five broad approaches: size, qualitative analysis, analysis of use, the extent to which electronic resources are used, and use of print journals.

### Size

The total size of a library's collection as reflected in a simple count is an often-asked question and provides a rough surrogate measure of the size of a library's operations. But the actual size of a collection reveals nothing about the adequacy of the collection to meet the information needs of a library's clients.

In prior years, standards would often dictate a minimum collection size, but clearly such an approach does little to address the real issue, which is what size collection will enable the library to provide an appropriate level of service. As noted previously, formulas have been developed in academic library settings, which are one tool in establishing a minimum collection size.

If a library must rely heavily on document delivery and/or interlibrary loan, then its collection may be too small. Three measures that examine this possibility are the

- ratio of borrowings (ILL or Doc Delivery) to holdings (by subject);
- collection balance indicator: number of acquisitions + document delivery as a percent of collection (by subject); and
- over the copyright limit: number of requests for a journal that exceed the copyright limit.

### Qualitative Analysis

A qualitative analysis is an impressionistic technique. The library could invite knowledgeable librarians or users in specific disciplines to review and comment on the adequacy of a library's collection.

## *Analysis of Use*

Libraries have used a number of measures to examine the extent of collection utilization. Among these are the following:

- **Circulation statistics.** A variety of circulation reports can be produced by an automated library system. One frequently used measure is the ratio of the annual circulation compared to the total collection. This ratio is typically called the collection turnover rate. For example, 20,000 items loaned from a total collection of 50,000 volumes provides a collection turnover ratio of two-fifths or 40 percent.

- **In-library materials use.** In a similar manner, a library can track the use of materials within the library but not borrowed by the client. Some libraries may find that in-library use of materials may be equivalent to materials borrowed.

- **Collection sample.** The library can select a random sample of items and determine the last time the item was circulated (provided the item has a visible way to indicate this information, for example, a date due stamp). Often this information is organized based on the age of the item (year published).

- **Checkout sample.** Some automated systems will produce a report indicating the total number of times an item has circulated, circulated in the last year, and so forth.

- **Last circulation date.** The last circulation date can be used as a measure of the likelihood that an item will be borrowed again. A number of aging studies indicate that use declines with age. The "collection 80/20 rule" seems to apply: 80 percent of use occurs with the newest 20 percent of the collection.

- **Accessibility (weeding).** Several studies indicate that if a collection is weeded on a regular basis, use of the collection will increase. (Clients are more likely to find something of value when they are browsing.) Two popular ways to accomplish weeding are to use

  - Slote analysis: time since item's last circulation is used as a measure for weeding; or

  - CREW (Continuous Review, Evaluation, and Weeding): age of item, last use date, and MUSTY (misleading, ugly, superseded, trivial, and no use in your collection).

- **Materials availability.** Every client coming to the library or visiting the library's Web site is surveyed. The survey asks whether clients found what they were looking for, and if not, to provide as much information about the item or topic as possible. This information is then used to determine the "point of failure." As shown in Figure 3.1, there can be a number of reasons why clients are unable to find what they are looking for. Typically each of these factors is expressed as a percentage. As the client proceeds down the "decision tree" there is a success or failure for each factor. For example, no library is going to have everything that a client is seeking (the "just-in-case" versus "just-in-time" dilemma). This is sometimes called a "collection failure" and is expressed, for example, as "5 percent collection failure."

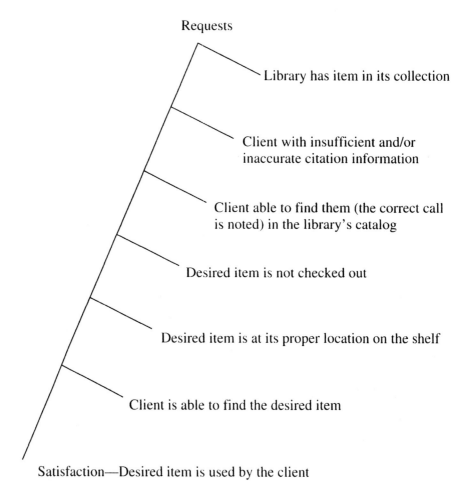

Requests

Library has item in its collection

Client with insufficient and/or inaccurate citation information

Client able to find them (the correct call is noted) in the library's catalog

Desired item is not checked out

Desired item is at its proper location on the shelf

Client is able to find the desired item

Satisfaction—Desired item is used by the client

**Figure 3.1. Availability Measures. Adapted from Paul B. Kantor.** *Objective Performance Measures for Academic and Research Libraries.* **Washington, DC: Association of Research Libraries, 1984. Reprinted with permission.**

## *Use of Electronic Resources*

The use of electronic journals and full-text databases is increasingly a fact of life in most special libraries. Use of these resources is typically evaluated using information about three factors, which are:

- **Cost.** What does a subscription for a particular journal title cost? More than likely the specific journal or journals of interest to a library will be bundled by the publisher or database provider so that the library has access to a greater number of electronic journals for a fixed price.

- **Use.** How frequently is the electronic journal or full-text database accessed and used by the library's clients? Most database vendors and publishers will provide reports indicating what resources are being used.

- **Fill rates.** A survey can be done to determine the ratio of the number of items found/the number of items sought.

One academic library found that the cost of a print title was $150, whereas an e-journal cost was $66 per title. The patrons of the academic library made more use of the e-journals, which therefore proved to be more cost effective.[6]

## *Print Journal Use*

Just as with electronic resources, the use of print journals is typically evaluated using the three measures: cost, use, and fill rates. Several studies have found that in-house use, circulation, and citation by researchers are all correlated. Use of print journals for educational and clinical purposes may not be reflected in research (citation by faculty researchers).

# Online Catalog Analysis Tools

As the principal finding tool for a library's collection, an effective online catalog is something that can pay rich dividends for the clients of the library. A successful online catalog search or access to electronic resources/databases (often provided as a part of the organization's intranet) depends on a number of factors:

- The accuracy of the information brought to the catalog by the user;

- The type of search performed by the user;

- The persistence of the user as evidenced by the use of multiple indexes and approaches in searching;

- The number of cross-references included in the database;

- The size of the database; and

- The usability of the catalog or search tool.

Among the methods that have been used successfully to evaluate online catalogs are the following:

- **Satisfaction surveys**. Starting with a major study of online catalogs funded by the Council on Library Resources in the early 1980s,[7] there has been a steady stream of studies that have used surveys to assess the success and satisfaction experienced by online catalog users.[8]

- **Transaction log analysis**. It is possible to use the computer to capture the interactions or transactions between the OPAC user and the computer. These transactions are subsequently analyzed to determine where the user is experiencing problems. These logs can also, for example, identify what types of searches failed as a percent of total searches. This information can then be used to explore changes to the user interface and the library's database so that the user is more successful. Some automated systems will also track what search terms failed (retrieved no records). This list of terms can then be sorted alphabetically and used as a source of cross-references.

- **Database analysis**. The library's bibliographic database can be analyzed to ensure that it will be most responsive when clients are searching. For example, the library could review all of its subject headings that are linked to too few or too many bibliographic records.

- **Usability testing**. The library could ask for a small number of clients to perform a series of tasks using a mockup of proposed changes to the library's online catalog. The library would ask these volunteers to verbally express what they are seeing and thinking as they work through the exercises. Based on the experiences of these individuals, the user interface could be revised and further testing can take place.

## Evaluation of Reference Services

A variety of factors will influence the quality of reference services provided in a library, including the skill, experience, and competencies of reference staff; staff attitudes toward clients; the reference collection size as well as the size of the general collection; the amount of bibliographic control (are authority files a part of the online catalog?); and the willingness of clients to seek reference assistance.

A variety of measures have been used to measure reference services. Among the more popular are the following:

- **Number of transactions**. A simple count of the number of questions asked is used both as an indication of the demand for the service and also to assist management in determining the staffing requirements at different times of the day. Often the count is separated into two groups: questions that can be answered in less than 10 minutes and those that take longer than 10 minutes. In other cases, the questions may be categorized, for example, directional and reference assistance questions.

- **Interviews**. A structured interview is used to assess whether the client's question was answered as well as his or her satisfaction with particular aspects of the reference service.

- **User satisfaction surveys**. This type of survey makes an assumption that if the client is satisfied with a service, in this case, reference, then the library has successfully met the client's needs. Although popular and easy to administer, a satisfaction survey is generally not a good method for determining the quality of reference services.

- **Unobtrusive measures**. An unobtrusive measure seeks to measure the quality of a service without the service provider being aware that he or she is being evaluated. Within reference, the best known unobtrusive study was conducted by Peter Hernon and Charles McClure. It resulted in the often-lamented and frequently cited 55 Percent Rule: Reference questions are answered completely and correctly about 55 percent of the time.[9] If 55 percent is not acceptable, what is acceptable? Is it 90 percent? Is it 75 percent? Does acceptable depend on the organizational setting? A law firm? A hospital library? A pharmaceutical library? A government research library? Charles Bourne has suggested that a library establish the 90 Percent Library as a goal.[10] In other words, the library should define an optimal, attainable goal and then periodically assess whether the library is reaching this goal.

Interestingly, the quality (as measured by the accuracy of the answer provided to a client's query) of reference service is influenced by the degree of interest shown by the reference librarian. The librarian who shows the least interest is likely to provide a correct answer about 33 percent of the time, whereas the librarian who shows the greatest interest will provide a correct answer about 76 percent of the time.[11]

# Document Delivery Evaluation

Libraries, and particularly special libraries, use a document delivery service to obtain copies of technical reports, standards, patents, legal materials, and other items to complement their existing collections. Although a commercial document delivery service may have an extensive collection of materials itself, typically these services contract with several libraries to supply copies of articles and other materials to the requesting library or individual. The revenues received by the commercial supplier for this service are split among the library supplying the material, the publisher for copyright permission, and the supplier itself. The measures typically used to evaluate a document delivery service include the following:

- **Speed**. How long does it take the document delivery supplier to respond and actually deliver the requested material to the library or the library's client? As various parts of the communication and handling process are automated, the delivery time decreases. As materials may be delivered via fax, e-mail, or overnight delivery, the speed is now expressed in hours rather than days.

- **Fill rate**. What proportion of the requests made by a library to a document delivery service are actually filled or delivered compared to the total number of requests? This proportion is usually expressed as a percent. Obviously, the library may need to contact another delivery service for those items the first document delivery service cannot fill. This adds to delays in the client receiving the material requested and adds to the library's overhead by handling the same request multiple times.

- **Cost**. The price for an item provided by a document delivery service will vary depending on the type of material and the length of the document itself.

- **Availability**. Some libraries will track the number of documents requested as a percent of collection size. Should this percentage become too large, then a library may complete an analysis to determine the subject area and type of documents being requested (and by implication, not found in the library's collection). This information can then be used to determine whether the acquisitions budget or selection policies should be revised.

Another measure is to compute the "collection balance indicator," which is a way to determine if a library is relying too much on document delivery. The collection balance ratio is determined using the following formula:

$$CB = \frac{Total\ acquisitions\ in\ class}{Total\ acquisitions} - \frac{Titles\ purchased\ in\ class}{Total\ titles\ purchased}$$

## Technical Services Evaluation

The evaluation of technical services is concerned principally with the efficiency of its operations. These process-oriented measures typically will answer such questions as: "What is the cost to acquire a title?" "What does it cost to catalog a title?" "What is the cost to receive a journal title?" Similar questions involve the time from receipt of a new title or journal title until it is placed on the shelf for use by the library's clients.

One useful measure is to determine how much overhead is consumed by the technical services operation. One such measure is the Technical Services Cost Ratio, or TSCORE. TSCORE is calculated by dividing the total salaries for technical services by the collection materials budget.

Some libraries have found that by flow charting their existing processes they can more readily identify the activities that consume the greatest amount of time, or bottlenecks that may exist.

## Facilities and Library Use

One obvious measure of the utility or value of a library is the degree to which it is used each day. For whatever reasons clients choose to visit the library, the fact that people are there is an indication, albeit an indirect measure, of the library's value. Among the measures that might be employed in this area are the following:

- **Attendance**. Counts per day of individuals entering the library (gate counts).

- **Facilities use rate**. Proportion of time the facility is busy compared to the total number of hours the library is open.

- **Building use**. Average number of people in the library per hour.

- **Service point queuing**. Are there times during the day when clients need to wait to be served? For example, do people have to wait at the reference desk or the circulation counter? This information can be helpful in scheduling staff to minimize the wait time of clients.

- **Remote use**. The library can track the number of log-ins to its library Web site and the library's online catalog. Use of specific electronic resources can also be tracked.

# PERFORMANCE MEASURES FOR GOVERNMENT LIBRARIES

Federal agencies may need to comply with the 1993 Government Performance and Results Act (GPRA). The purpose of this Act is to get managers to focus on achieving measurable results. Thus, libraries that are part of a federal government agency may want to develop and measure, on an ongoing basis, the value of their library services.

# INTERNATIONAL STANDARD

An international standard, ISO 11620, has been developed that identifies performance indicators for all types of libraries. This standard has been divided into two areas: public services and technical services. The 29 measures cover only traditional library services (the standard is currently being revised to include measures of electronic services):

User satisfaction

General (four measures of use/cost)

Providing documents (six measures of availability/cost)

Retrieving documents (two indicators of retrieval times)

Lending documents and document delivery (six measures of use/cost)

Inquiry and reference service (one measure of "correct answer" fill rate)

Information searching (two measures of catalog search success)

Facilities (four measures of availability/use)

Acquiring and processing documents (two measures on median times)

Cataloging (one indicator on cost per title)

# SUMMARY

As shown in this chapter, there are a variety of evaluation methodologies that can be used, depending on the purposes of the evaluation. A librarian, regardless of the size of the library, can implement most of these evaluation approaches. The key with any evaluation methodology is to make sure that the approach will yield information that will be helpful for the librarian or the intended decision maker.

# NOTES

1. Peter Drucker. *The Essential Drucker.* New York: HarperBusiness, 2001.

2. Priscilla Salant and Don A. Dillman. *How to Conduct Your Own Survey.* New York: John Wiley, 1994.

3. Peter Hernon and Robert E. Dugan. *An Action Plan for Outcomes Assessment in Your Library.* Chicago: American Library Association, 2002.

4. V. W. Clapp and R. T. Jordan. Qualitative Criteria for Adequacy of Academic Library Collections. *College and Research Libraries*, 26, 1965, 371–80.

5. For more information about the measures used and their associated weights to construct the HAPLR Index, visit the Web site, http://www.haplr-index.com.

6. Linda Mercer. Measuring the Use and Value of Electronic Journals and Books. *Issues in Science and Technology Librarianship*, 25, Winter 2000. Available at http://www.ucsb.edu/ist/00-winter/article1.html (accessed July 9, 2002).

7. Joseph R. Matthews, Ed. *The Impact of Online Catalogs.* New York: Neal-Schuman, 1986; and Joseph R. Matthews, Gary S. Lawrence, and Douglas K. Ferguson, Eds. *Using Online Catalogs: A Nationwide Survey. A Report of a Study Sponsored by the Council on Library Resources.* New York: Neal-Schuman, 1983.

8. Christine L. Borgman. Why Are Online Catalogs Hard to Use? Lessons Learned From Information Retrieval Studies. *Journal of the American Society for Information Science*, 37 (6), June 1986, 387–90; and Christine L. Borgman. Why Are Online Catalogs Still Hard to Use? *Journal of the American Society for Information Science*, 47 (7), July 1996, 493–503.

9. Peter Hernon and Charles R. McClure. Unobtrusive Reference Testing: The 55 Percent Rule. *Library Journal*, 111 (8), April 15, 1986, 37–41.

10. Charles P. Bourne. Some User Requirements Stated Quantitatively in Terms of the 90 Percent Library, in Allen Kent and Orrin E. Taulbee (Eds.). *Electronic Information Handling*. Washington, DC: Spartan, 1965, 93–110.

11. R. Gers and L. J. Seward. Improving Reference Performance: Results of a Statewide Study. *Library Journal*, 110 (18), 1985, 32–35.

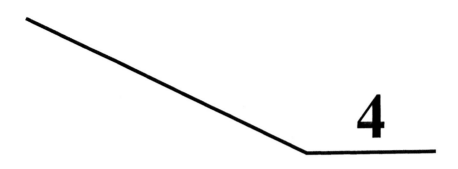

# 4

# Input Measures

*Sometimes what counts can't be counted,*
*and what can be counted doesn't count.*

—Albert Einstein

Historically, libraries have used input measures as performance indicators, in part because they are relatively easy to collect and report. Input measures reflect the resources that are available to support the operation of the library (see Figure 4.1). The measures will answer such questions as: "How much?" "How many?" In some cases, an input measure is called a capacity measure. A capacity measure describes the ability of a library to provide access to an electronic service. For example, the number of Internet workstations would be a capacity measure.

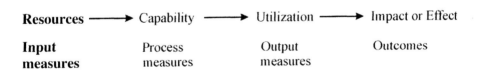

Resources ⟶ Capability ⟶ Utilization ⟶ Impact or Effect

**Input**       Process       Output       Outcomes
**measures**     measures     measures

**Figure 4.1. Evaluation Model**

# STANDARDS

A standard, as found in the engineering, scientific, manufacturing, or military communities, is the set of specifications or criteria used to measure the quality, shape, or other characteristics of a specific product or process. To be effective, a standard cannot be open to a great deal of interpretation or variance. Walt Crawford suggests that there are four broad types of standards: rules and regulations, goals and performance standards, qualitative standards, and technical standards.[1] For purposes of this discussion, a fifth category has been added to Crawford's four types of standards:

- **Accreditation**. Accreditation standards are set by an outside organization and represent the minimum standard that must be met before the "benefit" of accreditation is conferred. Colleges and universities are accredited on a regular basis. The American Library Association confers an accreditation to library schools. A degree from such an accredited library school, often referred to as "a MLS degree from an ALA-accredited school," is supposed to have greater value than a degree from a nonaccredited school. In some cases, reference is made in employment ads that the employer is seeking "a librarian with a MLS degree from an ALA-accredited school."

- **Rules and guidelines**. Personnel standards are guidelines that refer to such issues as the kind of education required to perform a job, that is, type and level of college degree, certification in a particular discipline, years of experience, and so forth. *The Anglo-American Cataloguing Rules*, second edition, establishes a set of rules for descriptive cataloging.

- **Goals and performance standards**. Performance standards are quantitative measures that assist in the process of comparing or benchmarking one library with others. An international standard, ISO 11620, contains some performance measures for libraries.

- **Qualitative standards**. Qualitative or projective standards are intended to provide guidelines for the development of library services. Since the 1930s, librarians have been involved in establishing projective standards for all types of libraries: public,[2] academic,[3] school, and special.[4] Yet almost from the outset, these "library standards" were beset by controversy and were often viewed as unenforceable guidelines, generalities, or objectives. To a large extent, these library standards were composed of input measures dealing with such issues as budgets, staffing, space, size of collection, and so forth.

  It would also be fair to say that these "projective standards" were not objective and thus failed even the broadest possible definition of the word "standard." Frequently projective library standards were criticized because:

–The choice of measures and the establishment of threshold values were arbitrary. Phrases such as "generalizations," "vague and wordy," "recommended practices and not standards," "guidelines or a checklist," and "reference points" were used by some to describe and criticize the library standards.

–Some measures were descriptive, making evaluation thorny.

–They failed to recognize unique characteristics and needs of a user population.

–They focused on input measures rather than assisting in identifying the outcomes of the library.[5]

After more than 50 years of effort, as chronicled in a rich and extensive literature,[6] as well as a number of attempts to produce standards for every type of library, the library profession has finally abandoned efforts to establish proscriptive library standards and has moved to the more important question of identifying the impact that the library has on its community or parent organization.

- **Technical standards**. Technical standards are the area where all types and sizes of libraries of libraries have benefited. Examples of these standards include Z39.2 (Bibliographic Information Interchange, more commonly referred to as the MARC record format) and Z39.50 (making it possible to retrieve information from dissimilar computer systems).

# TYPES OF INPUT MEASURES

In general, there are five broad categories of input measures:

- **Budget**. Measures in this category are focused on the library's finances. Although knowing the total budget of another library allows one to determine if a library is roughly similar in terms of size of operations, the amount of the total budget reveals little. Knowing the total budget in conjunction with other budget-related input measures can provide additional perspectives and insights. Some of the more frequently used input measures are

–Total budget of the library,

–Budget expenditures per professional staff member in the organization,

–Budget expenditures per library customer,[7] and

–Budget expenditures for acquisitions.

- **Staffing**. The budget allows the library to hire staff and provide services. Among the more popular staff-related input measures are

    –Total library staff (full-time equivalent, or FTE),

    –Total number of librarians (FTE),

    –Total number of paraprofessionals,

    –Number of actual library clients per librarian, and

    –Number of professionals in the organization compared to the number of librarians. For example, there might be 250 professionals per librarian.[x]

- **Collection**. Over the course of time the library is able to build and maintain its collection. Collection input measures include

    –Size of the collection—number of titles;

    –Size of the collection—number of volumes;

    –Size of the reference collection;

    –Size of the collection—by subject area, call number range; and

    –Net growth rate of the collection—number of titles, volumes.

- **Library information system**. The automated library information system is viewed as a requirement because access to the network infrastructure and a variety of information resources is no longer optional. As such the automated system is viewed as an input, and measures reflecting this fact include

    –Total dollars spent on the maintenance of the automated system (dollars to the vendor plus staff costs),

    –Annual automated system maintenance costs as a percent of the total library's budget,

    –Number of staff workstations,

    –Number of online catalog workstations (in the library),

    –Speed of network connection for each workstation, and

    –Speed of connection to the Internet.

- **Space**. The amount of space provided to the library to house the library's collection, staff, and automated system resources that enable the library to provide its services is an indirect input measure. Among the space-related measures are

    –Total space—square feet and

    –Space per square foot per professional within the organization.

The more frequently used input measures are shown in Appendix A.

The principal problem with input measures is that they provide information about the library without any context. Consider a library with a collection of 40,000 volumes. Without knowing more about the parent organization, having that information about the collection size is simply a data point and, by itself, not very helpful.

## SUMMARY

Not surprisingly, librarians first used input measures in an attempt to communicate the value of the library and its information services. However, as noted in this chapter, reliance on input measures alone does not begin to convey the real contribution of a special library.

## NOTES

1. Walt Crawford. *Technical Standards: An Introduction for Librarians*. 2nd ed. Boston: G. K. Hall, 1991.

2. American Library Association. *Public Library Service: A Guide to Evaluation with Minimum Standards*. Chicago: American Library Association, 1956; L. Carnovsky. Public Library Surveys and Evaluations. *Library Quarterly*, 25, 1955, 23–36; F. B. Murray. Canadian Library Standards. *Library Trends*, 21, 1972, 298–311; and Public Library Association, Professional Standards Committee. *Minimum Standards for Public Library Systems*. Chicago: American Library Association, 1967.

3. Association of College and Research Libraries. Standards for College Libraries. *College and Research Libraries*, 20, 1959, 274–80; Association of College and Research Libraries. Standards for Junior College Libraries. *College and Research Libraries*, 21, 1960, 200–26; F. E. Hirsch. Raising the Standards: College Libraries. *Drexel Library Quarterly*, 2, 1966, 199–201; and F. T. Jones. The Regional Accrediting Association and the Standard for College Libraries. *College and Research Libraries*, 22, 1961, 271–74.

4. Special Library Association. Professional Standards Committee. Objectives and Standards for Special Libraries. *Special Libraries*, 55, December 1964, 672–80.

5. Appraisals of "Objectives and Standards for Special Libraries." *Special Libraries*, 56, March 1965, 197–201.

6. For an extensive review of the history of library standards, see F. W. Lancaster. *The Measurement and Evaluation of Library Services*. Washington, DC: Information Resources Press, 1977, chapter 10.

7. In 1993, the average special library expenditures per customer were $1,700. Jose-Marie Griffiths and Donald W. King. *Special Libraries: Increasing the Information Edge*. Washington, DC: Special Libraries Association, 1993.

8. Jose-Marie Griffiths and Donald W. King, reported an average of 166 professionals in the organization per special library staff member. Ibid.

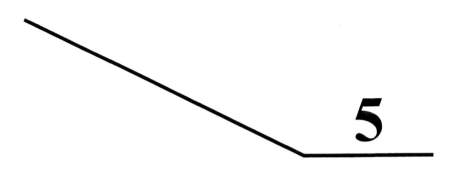

# 5

# Process Measures

*Things should be made as simple as possible,*
*but not any simpler.*

—Albert Einstein

Process or efficiency measures are really designed to answer the question, "Are we doing *things* right?" The library takes the resources provided as inputs and converts them into procedures and processes to be able to provide services (see Figure 5.1.). A large number of the decisions in a library revolve around cost. How much does it cost? Which is the best alternative? How do our costs relate to comparable libraries? Process measures are concerned with what is done rather than what is achieved.

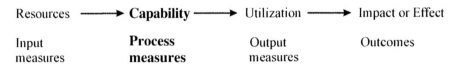

Resources ⟶ **Capability** ⟶ Utilization ⟶ Impact or Effect

| Input | **Process** | Output | Outcomes |
| measures | **measures** | measures | |

**Figure 5.1. Evaluation Model**

The majority of process measures will include cost and activity components, for example, the cost of cataloging per title or the cost of ordering per title. Process measures are designed to help a library improve operations and for reporting purposes. Just as input measures were sorted into categories, it is possible to separate process measures into three groups:

- **Efficiency**. The focus with this set of process measures is, how economical is this particular activity? How economical is the technical services operation? What is the cost per transaction to provide reference services, document delivery, and any other specific service?

- **Staff productivity**. Measures of staff productivity focus on the time it takes to complete a task or activity, for example, the time to complete copy cataloging, time for physical processing, or time to receive a journal. The staff productivity measures are independent of a particular technology; that is, staff could be using a manual system or an automated library system.

- **Library information system activity**. Automated system process measures are focused on system reliability measures, for example, system availability as expressed as a percent of uptime (99.9 percent) or system reliability as expressed as a percent of downtime (1.1 percent).

A list of the more frequently used process measures is included in Appendix A. Because a great many of these measures involve costs, the topic of activity based costing is addressed in the next section.

# ACTIVITY BASED COSTING

Activity based costing (ABC) is a method for accurately distributing all costs, including normally unassigned overhead costs, to activities (in the case of a library, the activity would be a service or supporting process such as cataloging). It will reveal the link between performing a particular activity and the demand that activity makes on an organization's resources.[1] It should also be noted that products and services do not consume overhead resources equally. A service organization, such as a library, presents a challenge for identifying and allocating costs because these organizations provide a service and not a product.

A library's "product" and services are, for the most part, intangible, that is, not a material good. And in some cases, the library's services can be consumed at the same place and at the same time, for example, two individuals simultaneously searching the library's catalog.

The first step involved in ABC is identifying all of the activities or tasks involved in a particular process or function. Information must be gathered and then analyzed. Some people find that preparing a flow chart helps them in both documenting the process and also understanding the relationships that exist between each of the tasks. One effective technique is for library staff to physically perform an activity while describing it to an interviewer. The extent and quantity of information gathered should be proportional to the benefits that will be received from performing the analysis.

# Types of Costs

Accountants typically place costs into one of two categories, direct or indirect. *Direct costs* in a library, for example, would be the salaries of the staff, expenses to acquire books and other library materials, supplies, and licenses for online databases.

*Indirect costs*, sometimes called overhead, may be shared with other parts of the organization. For example, administrative services, personnel, fringe benefits for all employees of an organization, information technology, purchasing, maintenance, utilities, and other services benefit all departments of an organization. Recognizing the existence of indirect costs and then distributing these costs fairly among the departments that use the service is an important part of preparing a cost analysis.

Costs can also be divided into fixed, semi-fixed, variable, and semi-variable:

- **Fixed costs** are those that remain the same, regardless of the level of activity, for example, salaries of some key employees, insurance, or rent.

- **Semi-fixed or semi-variable costs** have both fixed and variable components. For example, utilities such as electricity or telephone service often have a fixed minimum monthly charge plus additional fees based on usage.

- **Variable costs** are those that vary in direct proportion to the volume of activity. If the library uses an online database that charges solely on the basis of connect time, then obviously the more it is used, the higher the charges that will be incurred by the library.

Accounting reports typically provide an after-the-fact, historical view of what is happening within the organization. If these chart-of-account expenses can be translated into the work activities being performed by the organization, the value to a manager will increase substantially. In addition, the chart-of-accounts does not report on the true business process costs, which cross functional or departmental boundaries. Activity based costing segments and traces work activity costs to give a better picture of the actual costs to provide a service. The information provided by an ABC analysis forms the foundation for a number of performance measurement systems and allows the library to have a better idea of how its inputs are being transformed into outputs.

An activity that causes costs to vary, that is a variable cost or a semi-variable cost, is called a cost driver.[2] Using the information initially gathered about a function or activity, perhaps reviewing the work flow chart, will identify the underlying cost driver of an activity. It should be noted that labor is the result of a demand for a service and is not to be considered a cost driver. Table 5.1 (page 48) illustrates the cost drivers for some typical activities. One of the real benefits of activity based costing is that it helps library management gain a better understanding of what causes costs to be incurred.

## Table 5.1. Cost Drivers

| Activity | Cost Driver |
|---|---|
| Receiving journals/newspapers | Number of print journal subscriptions |
| Technical services | Number of titles ordered |
| Circulation services | Number of items borrowed |
| Receiving and processing of new materials | Number of titles ordered |
| Document delivery service | Number of items ordered |
| Online search service | Number of online searches |
| Reference service | Number of reference questions |
| Personnel services | Number of new hires/number of openings |

# Personnel Costs

Due to the labor-intensive nature of a library, personnel costs often consume a major portion of a library's budget. Thus, having a clear notion of the actual costs for each staff member will be an important part of any cost analysis.

Consider a staff member named Sue who has an annual salary of $40,000. Although dividing the annual salary by 2,000 hours (approximate number of hours worked in a year) will yield an hourly rate of $20.00, this rate ignores a number of other important considerations.

The fringe benefits received by an employee will vary depending on the type of organization and a number of other factors. Among the more typical fringe benefits are Social Security, health insurance, life and disability insurance, and a retirement plan. For the purposes of this discussion, we will assume a fringe benefit rate of 40 percent. Thus, Sue's total salary costs would be $56,000 based on a calculation of $40,000 + $16,000 (40 percent of $40,000). Sue's hourly rate would now be $28.00.

However, including the fringe benefits still does not reflect the true picture. So far the calculations have ignored the fact that Sue receives a vacation, has sick and personal leave days, and is not expected to work on holidays. Subtracting 25 days from 260 days (52 weeks/year) yields 235 actual work days. In addition, Sue takes two 15-minute breaks each day, meaning that Sue really works 7.5 hours per day or 1,763 hours per year. This yields an hourly rate of $31.76.

In addition, Sue must attend a number of library staff meetings, and she participates in other nonproductive activities that total some 150 hours per year. Thus, Sue's real hourly rate would be $34.72. This is almost 75 percent more than our first rough estimate of the cost of Sue's time.

## Cost Analysis

The goal of any cost analysis is to ensure that all of the cost components are included and accurately accounted for. Once the costs for a process or activity have been determined, it is often necessary to divide the total costs with a volume of associated activity to calculate the average cost per activity.[3] Examples include the cost to place an order, the cost to receive a journal issue, the cost to loan an item, and the cost to provide reference services.

In other cases, it may be necessary to calculate the costs, and perhaps the benefits, associated with several alternatives. In sum, the ability to accurately prepare a cost analysis is the foundation for meaningful and well-informed decisions about the library and its operations. Cost analysis is also the foundation for benchmarking.

# BENCHMARKING

Benchmarking is an organized process for measuring products, services, and practices against external partners to achieve improved performance. Since benchmarking requires considerable time and resources to complete, it must be done for a process or service within the library that is important, especially if it is important for the clients of the library. After learning how well a library does it now, one learns from others how they do it and then applies what has been learned to make the library's operations or service better. The process of benchmarking is often associated with the phrase "best practices."

Although it is possible to partner with a department within one's own organization, more frequently benchmarking studies select external partners that are within the same industry or an external partner known for its excellence in an area or process that is not a part of one's industry. In some benchmarking studies, a library will select external partners within the same industry as well as nonindustry external partners. This provides a greater breadth of experience and allows the library to achieve productivity improvements greater than can be obtained by, for example, only selecting partners from within the same industry.[4]

Aside from improving the productivity and performance of the library service, benchmarking demonstrates to upper management the library's commitment to providing quality services that have value to the organization. There are two types of benchmarking:

- **Performance benchmarking** answers the question: "What is best performance and how do we compare with the partners involved in the study?" Typically this type of benchmarking involves only the exchange of several performance measures and no on-site visits.

- **Process benchmarking** answers the question: "How can we identify and learn from leading practitioners in specific business processes?" The objective is to visit a number of partners to both gather data and to understand the logic and objectives of the workflows in a particular organization.

According to Holly Muir, benchmarking normally involves a five-step process:

1. **Conduct a preliminary analysis**. The needs of three groups should be addressed: upper management (What are their expectations?), library clients (What functions or services do they deem important?), and library staff members (What service or process do they feel needs to be improved?).

2. **Develop process measures**. After identifying what to benchmark, the library must first understand what it currently does and how well it is doing it. Tools that may be used to understand the current processes include a work process chart (which lists all of the activities, and who performs them, needed to complete the process), a flow chart, and/or a fishbone diagram. At this point the library should identify the performance measures it would like to use to gauge the same process in the partner organizations. Normally three to seven measures are used.

3. **Identify partners**. Partners may include libraries in the same industry, for example, law libraries, as well as other libraries outside the industry. (Check the literature for libraries that employ library "experts.") Potential partners outside the library industry include bookstores, video stores, information brokers, and museums.

4. **Collect and analyze the data**. If the primary focus of the benchmarking study is to better understand the process used in the partner organization, then site visits may be appropriate. (This adds considerably to the time and cost of such a project.) Otherwise, all that may be needed is to exchange data using the performance measures previously identified.

5. **Present results to management**. Prepare a written report that documents the benchmarking study. A typical succinct report documenting the resulting of the benchmarking study would include the following:

   –Executive summary,

   –Background information—what was benchmarked and why,

   –Performance measures used,

   –Results—library data compared to partner data, and

   –Recommendations—actions taken so far.[5]

One of the most obvious caveats to be observed about benchmarking, given its cost, is to make sure that the likely benefits will be sizable. Clearly benchmarking a process or service that is little used will have minimal overall impact on the library and its clients. Some of the benefits that result from benchmarking are

- The improved understanding of workflows, processes, and procedures;
- The discovery of new ideas that lead to continuous improvement or significant change;
- A new perspective on workflows, processes, and procedures used by other organizations;
- Improved productivity;
- Better appreciation by library staff of their customers;
- Reduction in turnaround times to complete a task or activity;
- Higher regard of library customers for staff members; and
- An appreciation by library staff that they can contribute to continuous improvement.

When examining a process within a library for potential improvements in quality and reducing costs, the library should consider ways to

- Eliminate steps or activities that do not add value,
- Consider adding activities that do add value,
- Redesign the steps in the process,
- Understand the difference between time to add value and cycle time (time to complete a process),
- Improve the skills of staff through additional training,
- Introduce more efficient technologies,
- Restructure the mix of staff to better use staff time,
- Examine the scheduling of staff to better handle the peaks and valleys of work demands, and
- Consider outsourcing to a more cost-efficient provider.

# SCOPE OF CHANGE

Any activity to effect change within a library, including benchmarking, is going to be influenced by the vision for the planned project. Efforts to make changes in a library or any organization are limited in two ways. First, changes are dictated by the scope of the anticipated or planned change. As shown in Figure 5.2 (page 52), a planned project can focus on a particular module or subprocess (for example, preparation of material orders) or assume a broader perspective (department or the complete organization). Second, the change can be radical or incremental:

- **Sweeping innovation.** In some cases, an organization will attempt to perform "radical" surgery in an attempt to significantly reduce costs or improve productivity for a single process or activity. In these cases, the process is viewed from all aspects and the focus is to eliminate departmental "silos" from hampering the planned improvements.

- **Business concept innovation.** This category of change takes the broadest possible perspective, typically organizationwide, and attempts to create a new organizational structure and performance measurement system in an attempt to re-invent the business or service offerings. In some cases, dot.com start-ups, which are not hampered by existing organizational structures and tradition, have developed an approach to a market that completely rewrites the rules of competition.

    Business concept innovation is sometimes called business process reengineering. Dell Computer, Charles Schwab, Amazon.com, and GE Capital Finance are examples of companies where business concept innovation has been successfully applied.

- **Continuous improvement.** Activities that involve continuous improvement have a limited perspective and are making changes that will, over time, improve the productivity of some staff members and reduce the costs for performing a particular activity or process.

- **Business process improvement.** Rather than being limited to a single module or subprocess, business process improvement will examine the various tasks and activities that are being performed within a department or organization to determine what incremental improvements can be made to reduce costs and improve productivity.

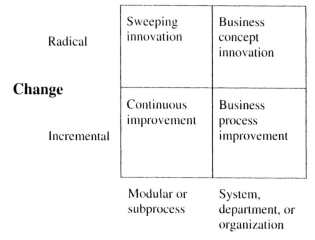

**Scope**

**Figure 5.2. Scope of Change**

# SUMMARY

Process measures are designed to reveal how efficient operations are within the library. The measures typically focus on the time and cost to perform a specific task or activity. For example, measures might indicate the time and cost to perform copy cataloging, original cataloging, and a combination of copy plus original cataloging. With this information in hand, the library can then compare its process measures with those of other comparable libraries to ensure that it is operating in an efficient manner.

# NOTES

1. Robin Cooper and Robert S. Kaplan. Profit Priorities for Activity-Based Costing. *Harvard Business Review*, 91, May/June 1991, 358–66.

2. Gene Danilenko. Activity Based Costing for Services: The Corporate Information Center. *Special Libraries*, 85 (1), Winter 1994, 24–29.

3. Madeline J. Daubert. *Analyzing Library Costs for Decision-Making and Cost Recovery*. Washington, DC: Special Libraries Association, 1997.

4. Robert C. Camp. *Benchmarking: The Search for Industry Best Practices That Lead to Superior Performance*. Milwaukee, WI: ASQC Quality Press, 1989; see also Robert C. Camp. *Business Process Benchmarking: The Search for Industry Best Practices that Lead to Superior Performance*. Milwaukee, WI: ASQC Quality Press, 1995; and Annette Gohlke. Benchmark for Strategic Performance Improvement. *Information Outlook*, 1 (8), August 1997, 22–24.

5. Holly J. Muir. *Conducting a Preliminary Benchmarking Analysis: A Librarian's Guide*. Cincinnati, OH: Library Benchmarking International, 1993; Holly J. Muir. *Developing Benchmarking Metrics: A Librarian's Guide*. Cincinnati, OH: Library Benchmarking International, 1993; Holly J. Muir. *Identifying Benchmarking Partners: Special Libraries*. Cincinnati, OH: Library Benchmarking International, 1993; Holly J. Muir. *Collecting & Analyzing Benchmarking Data: A Librarian's Guide*. Cincinnati, OH: Library Benchmarking International, 1993; and Holly J. Muir. *Presenting Benchmarking Results: A Librarian's Guide*. Cincinnati, OH: Library Benchmarking International, 1993.

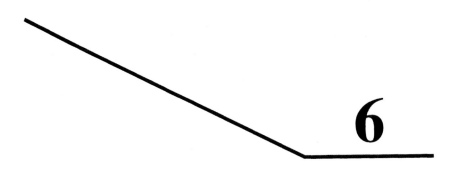

# 6

# Output Measures

*The last 10 percent of performance generates one-third of the cost and two-thirds of the problems.*

—Norman Augustine

Output measures describe the use or utilization of the library (see Figure 6.1). These measures are primarily descriptive in the sense that they reflect how frequently the library or a specific service is used. Among the questions that can be addressed by output measures are: How frequently was the service rendered? How well? How accurate was the information? How reliable was the information provided? How responsive was the library staff member? How courteous was the library employee? How satisfied was the client?

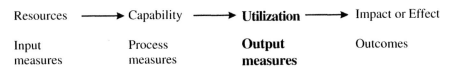

Resources   ⟶   Capability   ⟶   **Utilization**   ⟶   Impact or Effect

Input measures      Process measures      **Output measures**      Outcomes

**Figure 6.1. General Evaluation Model**

After several decades of focusing on library input measures and the struggles to adopt meaningful standards, the move to output measures was warmly welcomed by the library community since these measures reflected how much the library was being used. Output measures can be generated for a wide variety of library services and activities, as shown in Appendix A. However, it is possible to group these measures into five general categories:

- **Services**. Output measures for library services reflect the range of services offered and typically rely on counts and use per capita statistics. Examples of such library service-oriented output measures are number of documents requested from a document delivery service and number of reference questions answered.

- **Quality**. Output measures that concentrate on quality typically ask clients for feedback or an assessment of their satisfaction with a specific library service or of the library in general (the data for this feedback are most often gathered using a written satisfaction survey instrument). In addition, the use of unobtrusive methods to assess the "correctness" of reference services is another way to measure the quality of the service being provided. A subsequent section in this chapter discusses the advantages and disadvantages of using satisfaction measures.

- **Collection use**. Output measures that reflect the use of a library's collection are important for at least two reasons. First, these measures reflect the degree to which the library's collection of materials is being used. Second, use of these measures can assist in evaluating the degree to which the assembled collection of materials is meeting the needs of the clients. For example, if the turnover rate of a library's collection (annual circulation plus in-house use of materials divided by the total number of volumes) is low, then perhaps the collection is aging and no longer reflects the information needs of the potential clients from within the organization.

  The evaluation of the library's collection must include both its print collection as well as the electronic full-text resources to which the library provides access. Increasingly the library's catalog reflects not only the print resources housed in the library but also links to resources that may be found on the Internet. In addition, a great many online catalogs also provide access to citation/abstract and full-text databases that the library has licensed. In some cases, access to these online databases may be provided from a library's Web pages or information portal.

- **Online catalog/portal use**. The online catalog, often called the library OPAC, is the search engine that assists the library's clients in finding materials of potential value. A wide variety of measures can be used to determine the degree to which the chief finding aid for the library's collection is being successfully used.

- **Building activity**. In addition to providing access to a variety of information services, a library often has a number of other resources. For example, the library may provide meeting rooms, tables and chairs to perform research or reading, photocopiers, or the opportunity to browse the collection looking for something that might stimulate thinking to solve a problem.

Some have suggested that output measures have an outward focus, but in reality these measures reflect an inward orientation in that they measure how much the library is used and not the impact or effect of the library on the larger organization. Remember, there is no clear inherent or implied value in activity per se.

At times, a library may embark on a self-study or ask an outside consultant to assess it. Such studies are often referred to as library studies. Most library studies will use several methods and sources to gather data to prepare an analysis and come up with a set of recommendations. One of the tools often employed in a library study is a client satisfaction survey.

# SATISFACTION

Libraries have long relied on the use of satisfaction surveys as a means of gauging their success in meeting the needs of their clients. The assumption made with a satisfaction survey is that the client is in the best position to objectively assess the quality and utility of library services. In another sense, a satisfaction survey is a use study because the focus is on specific library services and of the general perceptions of the library. Typically the intent of the satisfaction survey is to ask the client to evaluate the effectiveness of the services provided, determine the extent to which the client's needs were met and, in some cases, identify ways to improve the service.

Given the potentially high costs associated with designing and administering the survey and analyzing the resulting data, the use of a satisfaction survey should be carefully assessed. Library staff can conduct satisfaction surveys, or an outside consultant may be employed. If an outside consultant is used, the results of the survey may have various advantages. The outside individual or organization may have more experience in designing and administering an "objective" survey, and the management team of the library may be more willing to act on the recommendations.

There are, of course, problems associated with conducting a satisfaction survey. The majority of these problems are technical, such as ensuring that an appropriate sample size is obtained, that the sample is randomly generated, and that the questions are appropriately worded.[1] Yet the biggest underlying problem associated with any survey, let alone a satisfaction survey, is making sure that the right questions are asked.

Satisfaction measures are designed to identify the net satisfaction with a product or service, and the observed distribution of satisfaction ratings is presumed to be a reflection of "true" satisfaction. However, in virtually all customer satisfaction surveys the distribution of responses is positively skewed, that is, the majority of the survey respondents report high levels of satisfaction (see Figures 6.2 and 6.3, page 58).[2] Libraries must recognize and deal with the fact that they are considered a "good thing"—much like apple pie and motherhood.[3] In addition, customer satisfaction data are often viewed as a report card rather than as a source of information about areas where improvement or further investigation is required. Companies have learned that only when customers rate their buying experience as completely or extremely satisfied can they count on the customers' repeat purchasing behavior.[4]

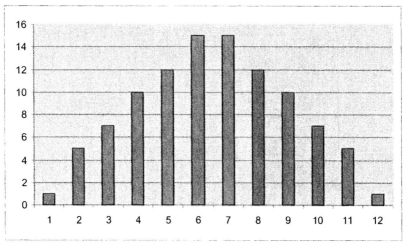

Figure 6.2. Normal Distribution

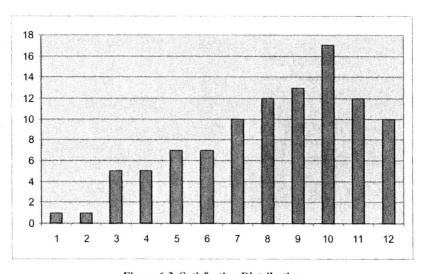

Figure 6.3. Satisfaction Distribution

# Priority Setting

Asking clients about the relevance of existing and possible library services is one form of a client satisfaction survey that can have immediate and positive impact. The clients will benefit since the library will clearly understand what services have the greatest positive impact on their personal or professional lives. The library, in turn, can benefit from such a survey in that it will identify what services are most important and also understand how the users rate the library's current performance for each service.

Marianne Broadbent popularized the use of a satisfaction survey methodology called priority and performance evaluation, or PAPE.[5] For each actual or possible library service, the client is asked to indicate the priority the library should give to each, using a Likert scale. Following this, the client is asked to rate the library's performance in providing the service. (See a sample PAPE survey instrument in Figure 6.4 and Appendix B.) In addition to asking clients to participate in a PAPE survey, seeking the participation of the managers within the larger organization as well as library staff will allow the library to compare and contrast the responses from these three important groups. Should any differences emerge among the three groups, then these differences obviously deserve further attention and consideration. One study found that although there was general congruence between library staff and their customers, there was a tendency for library staff members to underestimate the importance of performing the promised service dependably and accurately.[6]

---

In your opinion, what priority should the library give each of the following?
Please circle the number that best gives an indication of your assessment.

| | Low Priority | | | Very High Priority | | | Don't Know | |
| --- | --- | --- | --- | --- | --- | --- | --- | --- |
| | < | | | | | | > | |
| Availability and accessibility of library staff | 1 | 2 | 3 | 4 | 5 | 6 | 7 | D |
| Accuracy of information services | 1 | 2 | 3 | 4 | 5 | 6 | 7 | D |
| Timeliness of information services | 1 | 2 | 3 | 4 | 5 | 6 | 7 | D |
| Information alert service | 1 | 2 | 3 | 4 | 5 | 6 | 7 | D |
| Document delivery service | 1 | 2 | 3 | 4 | 5 | 6 | 7 | D |
| Access to online databases | 1 | 2 | 3 | 4 | 5 | 6 | 7 | D |

In your opinion, how well does the library perform in each of the following areas?
Please circle the number that best gives an indication of your assessment.

| | Low Priority | | | Very High Priority | | | Don't Know | |
| --- | --- | --- | --- | --- | --- | --- | --- | --- |
| | < | | | | | | > | |
| Timeliness of information services | 1 | 2 | 3 | 4 | 5 | 6 | 7 | D |
| Information alert service | 1 | 2 | 3 | 4 | 5 | 6 | 7 | D |
| Availability and accessibility of library staff | 1 | 2 | 3 | 4 | 5 | 6 | 7 | D |
| Access to online databases | 1 | 2 | 3 | 4 | 5 | 6 | 7 | D |
| Document delivery service | 1 | 2 | 3 | 4 | 5 | 6 | 7 | D |
| Accuracy of information services | 1 | 2 | 3 | 4 | 5 | 6 | 7 | D |

*Note:* The order of the library services in the second question should be different than the sequence of the first question. This forces the respondent to carefully read and rate each library service.

**Figure 6.4. Sample PAPE Questionnaire**

A sample of the results from a PAPE survey is shown in Figure 6.5. In all, 21 library services were prioritized and evaluated (identified using the letters of the alphabet). Notice that for the first 14 services, the priority assigned by the library's clients exceeded the library's ability to deliver the expected level of service (with three exceptions). For the services with lower priorities, actual performance exceeded expectations in only two cases. Yet some adjustment of the service levels for these two highly rated services might be warranted.

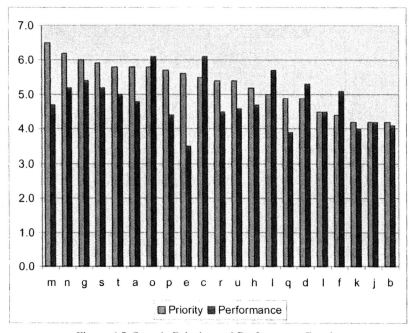

**Figure 6.5. Sample Priority and Performance Results**

Libraries that have used PAPE have found it to be a useful tool that can be administered periodically, for example annually, to capture any shifts of the priorities of their clients as well as tracking improvements in the services provided.

## Service Quality

The quality of library services has received much attention in the professional literature in the last few years. Satisfaction has been defined in a number of ways, but one frequent definition is "the emotional reaction to a specific transaction or service encounter."[7] Service quality is probably an antecedent of customer satisfaction, and higher quality service levels will result in increased customer satisfaction. Yet a client can visit the library and obtain an answer to a question and be unsatisfied due to an encounter with a specific staff member.

There are probably two perspectives for considering satisfaction. The first is *service encounter satisfaction*, which is the satisfaction or dissatisfaction experienced by the client with a specific service transaction. The second is *overall service satisfaction*, or the degree of client satisfaction or dissatisfaction based on multiple transactions or experiences.[8] It is likely that the overall service satisfaction is built up over time and is the result of numerous transactions of varying quality. Others have suggested that *customer satisfaction* refers to a specific transaction, whereas *service quality* is the cumulative judgment based on all of the previous encounters.

All customers make certain assumptions when they purchase a product or receive a service, including the following:

- **Basic expectations** are a set of assumptions about the product or service that the customer never states. Failure to meet the basic expectations in terms of timeliness, accuracy of information, and so forth will lead to serious problems.

- **Spoken requirements** are those aspects of the service transaction that are explicitly stated by the customer. Asking questions of the customer will allow staff to make explicit some or all of the stated requirements.

- **Delight factors** are the unspoken requirements which, if provided, result in the customer being pleasantly surprised. If the customer expects a response to a query in one working day and a response is provided a few hours later, that will be a delight for the customer. Asking customers, perhaps in a focus group or using other tools, to respond to such questions as "How do you use this type of information?" "What could the library do to make this outcome better?" may allow library staff to learn what will delight their customers.

One popular service quality assessment tool, developed in the retail industry, that has been adapted for libraries and information services is called SERVQUAL (Service Quality).[9] SERVQUAL compares the expectations and performance using five attributes:

1. **Tangibles.** Physical appearance of the library, library staff members, equipment, and communication materials (signage, handouts, and so forth).

2. **Reliability.** Is the service dependable and accurate? This is the *most* important factor among the five attributes being evaluated by the client.

3. **Responsiveness.** How prompt is the service? Are staff members willing to provide assistance?

4. **Assurance.** Do staff convey trust and confidence? Are staff knowledgeable and courteous?

5. **Empathy.** Is the staff member providing individualized attention to the client?

A shorter, competing survey instrument, called SERVPERF (Service Performance), only asks the respondents to indicate their assessment of the service performance and does not ask for the respondent's expectations.[10]

Versions of SERVQUAL have been used in a number of libraries with some success.[11] One adaptation of SERVQUAL, named LibQUAL+, has been undergoing pilot testing by the Association of Research Libraries since the spring of 2000. Five dimensions were originally identified as being useful for assessing library service: affect of service, reliability, library as place, provision of physical collections, and access to information.[12] Further refinement of the LibQUAL+ instrument has found that there are four dimensions to the concept of library service quality: affect of service (responsiveness, assurance, empathy, and dependability), library as place (appearance of physical facilities, equipment, personnel, and communications materials), personal control (of the information universe and Web navigation), and information access (completeness of a library's collection, access to databases, and document delivery), as shown in Figure 6.6.[13] The LibQUAL+ survey instrument, administered using a Web-based form, is still being revised and tested. How it will be distributed for potential use by other libraries is still being discussed.

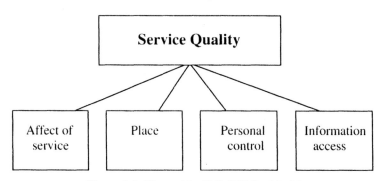

Figure 6.6. Hierarchical LibQUAL+ Model

It is possible to develop a generalized model of the interactions among and between client expectations, perceptions, satisfaction, their assessment of service quality, and the resulting overall customer satisfaction, as shown in Figure 6.7.

One of the real benefits of using SERVQUAL or any of the competing instruments is that data can be collected from different groups. For example, clients, the management team of the larger organization, and library staff could all be surveyed. An analysis of the differences and similarities in the ratings can be very revealing and helpful in assessing the quality of library services. Such an analysis might demonstrate that library staff feels they are providing excellent service while the clients and management team of the organization do not. This is due to the fact that these various survey instruments are assessing the "perceived quality" rather than attempting to determine an "objective measure of quality."

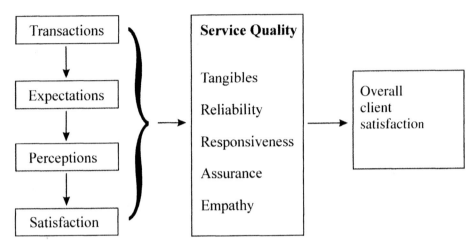

**Figure 6.7. Client Satisfaction and Service Quality Model. Adapted from "Perspectives on User Satisfaction Surveys" by Rowena Cullen, *Library Trends* Volume 49, Number 4, pp. 662–686. Copyright © 2001 The Board of Trustees of the University of Illinois. Reprinted with permission.**

In fact, use of SERVQUAL and of its competitors will reveal gaps between client expectations and perceptions. Five gaps may exist:

1. Discrepancy between client expectations and the library's perceptions of those expectations.

2. Difference between library's perceptions of client expectations and service quality specifications.

3. Variation between service quality specifications and actual service delivery.

4. Discrepancy between actual service delivery and what is communicated to clients about it.

5. Difference between client's expected service and perceived service delivered.[14]

The first four gaps contribute to gap 5, which is the difference between clients' expected service and perceived service delivered, sometimes called *customer sacrifice*. Although this latter gap is the primary focus of the research using the SERVQUAL surveys, the surveys do allow for an analysis of the other gaps. It is important to recognize that service quality really relates to expectations. And as Terry Vavra has noted,

- Expectations are *confirmed* when perceived performance meets them,
- Expectations are *affirmed* when perceived performance exceeds them, and
- Expectations are *disconfirmed* when perceived performance fails to meet them.[15]

# SUMMARY

Use of output measures, including satisfaction and service quality measures, can provide an important perspective on just how well the library is doing. Tracking the same measures over time allows the library to know if use of library services is declining or increasing. Given the large number of output measures that can be collected, the library needs to carefully assess what measures are most important so that busy staff are not overwhelmed with a data collection nightmare.

Using such tools as PAPE, the library can ask its clients to identify the services that are most highly valued. In turn, PAPE can assist in helping the library assess how it is doing from perhaps the most important perspective—that of the client.

# NOTES

1. Ray L. Carpenter and Ellen Storey Vasu. *Statistical Methods for Librarians.* Chicago: American Library Association, 1978. The reader might wish to consult an introductory text on statistics and survey research to learn more about the issues of sampling and the design of survey instruments. The use of a consultant in these areas might also be considered.

2. Douglas Badenoch, Christine Reid, Paul Burton, Forbes Gibb, and Charles Oppenheim. The Value of Information, in Mary Feeney and Maureen Grieves (Eds.)., *The Value and Impact of Information.* London: Bowker Saur, 1994, 9–78.

3. Ruth Applegate. Models of User Satisfaction: Understanding False Positives. *RQ,* 32 (4), 1993, 525–39.

4. T. O. Jones and W. E. Sasser. Why Satisfied Customers Defect. *Harvard Business Review,* November–December 1995, 88–99.

5. Marianne Broadbent and Hans Lofgren. Information Delivery: Identifying Priorities, Performance and Value, in OPAC and Beyond. Victorian Association for Library Automation 6th Biennial Conference and Exhibition. 11–13 November 1991, Hilton on the Park, Melbourne, Australia. 185–215; Marianne Broadbent. Demonstrating Information Service Value to Your Organization. *Proceedings of the IOLIM Conference,* 16, 1992, 65–83; and Marianne Broadbent and Hans Lofgren. *Priorities, Performance and Benefits: An Exploratory Study of Library and Information Units.* Melbourne, Australia: CIRCIT Ltd. and ACLIS, 1991.

6. Susan Edwards and Mairead Browne. Quality in Information Services: Do Users and Librarians Differ in their Expectations? *Library & Information Science Review*, 17, 1995, 163–82.

7. K. Elliott. A Comparison of Alternative Measures of Service Quality. *Journal of Customer Service in Marketing and Management*, I (1), 1995, 35.

8. Peter Hernon and Ellen Altman. *Assessing Service Quality: Satisfying the Expectations of Library Customers.* Chicago: American Library Association, 1998; see also Peter Hernon and Ellen Altman. *Service Quality in Academic Libraries.* Norwood, NJ: Ablex, 1996.

9. A. Parasuraman, Valarie A. Zeithaml, and Leonard L. Berry. SERVQUAL: A Multiple-Item Scale for Measuring Consumer Perceptions of Service Quality. *Journal of Retailing*, 64, 1988, 12–37; Valarie A. Zeithaml, A. Parasuraman, and Leonard L. Berry, *Delivering Quality Service: Balancing Customer Perceptions and Expectations.* New York: Free Press, 1990; and A. Parasuraman, Valarie A. Zeithaml, and Leonard L. Berry. Reassessment of Expectations as a Comparison Standard in Measuring Service Quality: Implications for Further Research. *Journal of Marketing*, 58 (1), January 1994, 111–24.

10. Joseph J. Cronin and Steven A. Taylor. SERVPERF versus SERVQUAL: Reconciling Performance-Based and Perceptions Minus Expectations of Service Quality. *Journal of Marketing*, 58 (1), January 1994, 125–31; see also Marilyn Domas White and Eileen G. Abels. Measuring Service Quality in Special Libraries: Lessons from Service Marketing. *Special Libraries*, Winter 1995, 36–45.

11. Syed S. Andaleeb and Patience L. Simmonds, Explaining User Satisfaction with Academic Libraries. *College and Research Libraries,* 59, March 1998, 156–67; Vicki Coleman, Yi (Daniel) Xiao, Linda Bair, and Bill Chollett. Toward a TQM Paradigm: Using SERVQUAL to Measure Library Service Quality, *College & Research Libraries,* 58, May 1997, 237–51; Susan Edwards and Mairead Browne. Quality in Information Services: Do Users and Librarians Differ in Their Expectations? *Library & Information Science Research,* 17, Spring 1995, 163–82; Danuda Nitecki. Changing the Concept and Measure of Service Quality in Academic Libraries. *Journal of Academic Librarianship,* 22 (3), 1996, 181–90; Ellen Altman and Peter Hernon. Service Quality and Customer Satisfaction Do Matter. *American Libraries,* 29 (7), 1998, 53–55; and Danuta Nitecki and Peter Hernon. Measuring Service Quality at Yale University's Libraries. *The Journal of Academic Librarianship* 26 (4), July 2000, 261.

12. Colleen Cook, Fred Heath, and Bruce Thompson. LibQUAL+: One Instrument in the New Measures Toolbox. Available at http://www.arl.org/newsltr/212/libqual.html (accessed July 9, 2002); Colleen Cook and Bruce Thompson. Higher-order factor analytic perspectives on users' perceptions of library service quality. *Library Information Science Research,* 22, 2000, 393–404; Colleen Cook and Bruce Thompson. Users' hierarchical perspectives on library service quality: A "LibQUAL+™" study. *College and Research Libraries,* 62, 2001, 147–53; Colleen Cook and Fred Heath. Users' Perceptions of Library Services Quality: A "LibQUAL+" Qualitative Study. *Library Trends,* 49, 2001, 548–84; .Bruce Thompson, Colleen Cook, and Russell L. Thompson. Reliability and Structure of LibQUAL+ Scores: Measuring Perceived Library Service Quality. *Portal: Libraries and the Academy,* 2 (1), 2002,

3–12; Colleen Cook, Fred Heath, and Bruce Thompson. Score Norms for Improving Library Service Quality: A LibQUAL+ Study. *Portal: Libraries and the Academy*, 2 (1), 2002, 13–26; .Fred Heath, Colleen Cook, Martha Kyrillidou, and Bruce Thompson. ARL Index and Other Validity Correlates of LibQUAL+ Scores. *Portal: Libraries and the Academy*, 2 (1), 2002, 27–42.

13. Carolyn A. Snyder. Measuring Library Service Quality with a Focus on the LibQUAL+ Project: An Interview with Fred Heath. *Library Administration & Management*, 16 (1), Winter 2002, 4–7.

14. A. Parasuraman, Valarie A. Zeithaml, and Leonard L. Berry. SERVQUAL: A Multiple-Item Scale for Measuring Consumer Perceptions of Service Quality. *Journal of Retailing*, 64, 1988, 12–37.

15. Terry G. Vavra. *Improving Your Measurement of Customer Satisfaction: A Guide to Creating, Conducting, Analyzing and Reporting Customer Satisfaction Management Programs.* Milwaukee: ASQ Quality Press, 1997, 42.

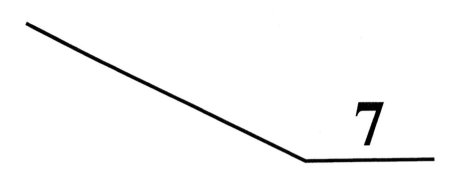

# Approaches to Identifying
# Outcomes or Impacts

*If we begin with certainties, we shall end with doubts;
but if we begin doubts, and are patient in them, we shall end
with certainties.*

—Francis Bacon

A wide variety of input, process, and output measures are available to a library to assess its performance. The widespread use of these measures means that a library can view itself from a number of perspectives. Historically, use of input, process, and output measures, as shown in Table 7.1 (page 68), has been a quantitative surrogate for relevance, quality, and value of a library and its information services. Given the plethora of such measures, how is it possible to choose what measure or set of measures to report to the managers who oversee the library? In addition, the question remains: Is it possible to assess the impact of the library in a larger context? What effect does a special library have on its larger organization?

## Table 7.1. Performance Measures

| Description | Input Measure | Process Measure | Output Measure |
|---|---|---|---|
| *Functional Activity:* | | | |
| Acquisitions | | | |
| • Efficiency | | Time to order and receive a title | |
| • Effectiveness | | | Acquisition orders roughly equal to circulation and in-library use (by subject area) |
| • Costs | Expenditure on acquisition of materials (and information) per professional<br><br>Acquisitions budget as a percent of the total budget | Average cost per item ordered | |
| • Productivity | | Number of items ordered per staff member | |
| Cataloging | | | |
| • Efficiency | | Cataloging turnaround time | |
| • Costs | | Cost per title added<br>Cost of copy cataloging<br>Cost of original cataloging | |
| • Productivity | | Total number of titles cataloged | |
| Circulation | | | |
| • Market penetration | | | Average number of loans per client/year |
| • Efficiency | | Accuracy of the service | Number of loans/service hour |
| • Effectiveness | | Time to shelve items | Total volumes loaned/year<br>Total in-library use/year |
| • Costs | | Cost per loan<br>Cost per service hour | |

| Description | Input Measure | Process Measure | Output Measure |
|---|---|---|---|
| • Productivity | | Number of loans/staff hour | |
| Serials (Print and Electronic) | | | |
| • Efficiency | Number of serials titles per number of professionals | Number of serial issues received annually/staff member | |
| • Effectiveness | | | Number of journals examined annually<br><br>Number of journal articles photcopied |
| • Cost | Cost of serial title subscriptions<br><br>Cost of serial subscriptions per professional | Average cost to receive serial issues | |
| *Library Services:* | | | |
| Catalog | | | |
| • Market penetration | | | Number of clients who use the catalog remotely/in the library |
| • Efficiency | | Library workstation hours used per month<br><br>Number of cross-references added per year | |
| • Effectiveness | | | Success rate of searching<br>—known item searches<br>—subject searches |
| • Cost | Number of catalog workstations | | |
| Collection | | | |
| • Efficiency | Volumes in collection per number of professionals | Cost of staff to select and weed collection/volumes added per year<br><br>Cost of staff to shelve/number of items shelved per year | Number of items used |

| Description | Input Measure | Process Measure | Output Measure |
|---|---|---|---|
| • Effectiveness | | Accuracy of shelving Time to retrieve an item | Availability rate |
| • Costs | Value of collection (average purchase price X number of volumes) | | |
| • Use | | | Collection turnover rate Items circulated/size of collection —by subject Percent of items circulated in last X years Percent of volumes not circulated in last X years |
| Current Awareness | | | |
| • Market penetration | Registered clients per total number of professionals | | |
| • Efficiency | | Cost of service per subscriber | |
| • Effectiveness | | | Client satisfaction survey Number of titles used by client compared to total number of citations received |
| • Productivity | | Number of "alerts" prepared per staff member | |
| Document Delivery | | | |
| • Market penetration | | | Number of clients who use document delivery per total number of professionals |
| • Efficiency | | Cost of service per request Number of requests filled/total number of requests | |
| • Effectiveness | | | Turnaround time |
| • Cost | Total cost of service as a percent of total library budget | Average cost per document received | |
| • Productivity | | Total number of requests/staff hour | |

| Description | Input Measure | Process Measure | Output Measure |
|---|---|---|---|
| Electronic Databases | | | |
| • Market penetration | | | Number of clients who access electronic databases per number of professionals |
| • Efficiency | Total number of databases<br><br>Total number of journal titles | Cost of service/ number of searches | Number of log-ins per professional |
| • Effectiveness | | | Number of documents<br>—retrieved<br>—examined (selected)<br>—downloaded<br>—printed |
| • Cost | Cost to license databases | Cost per log-in | |
| Interlibrary Loan | | | |
| • Market penetration | | | Number of clients who use ILL |
| • Efficiency | | Cost of service per request | Turnaround time |
| • Effectiveness | | | |
| Mediated Online Searching | | | |
| • Market penetration | Number of clients who use service per total number of professionals | | |
| • Efficiency | | Cost of service per search<br>Cost of service per client | Turnaround time |
| • Effectiveness | | | |
| Reference | | | |
| • Market penetration | Number of clients who use service per total number of professionals | | Percent of repeat use<br>Total number of searches |
| • Efficiency | | Inquiries answered/ service hour | Turnaround time |

| Description | Input Measure | Process Measure | Output Measure |
|---|---|---|---|
| • Effectiveness | | Percent of inquiries answered correctly | Percent of repeat use<br>Total number of reference transactions<br>Client satisfaction survey |
| • Costs | Cost of reference as percent of total library budget | Cost of service per transaction<br>Cost of service per client | |
| • Productivity | | Inquiries answered/ staff member | |
| **Overall Library Services:** | | | |
| Clients (Users) | Registered clients per total number of professionals | | Total active registered clients<br>Average number of visits/clients/year |
| Budget | Total library budget<br>Total library budget as percent of organization's total budget<br>Total library budget/number of professionals | Total library budget/service hour | |
| Facilities | | | |
| • Market penetration | Total space per professional | Average number of clients at a service point | Average number of clients in library at any point in time |
| • Efficiency | Number of seats in library<br>Total number of hours open per week | | Seat occupancy rate<br>Facilities use ratio |
| • Cost | Cost per square foot of library space<br>Cost per square foot of library space per professional | | |
| Information Technology | | | |
| • Efficiency | | System availability<br>Speed of network | |
| • Cost | IT expenditure as percent of total library budget | | |

| Description | Input Measure | Process Measure | Output Measure |
|---|---|---|---|
| Staff | | | |
| • Efficiency | Number of professionals/librarians<br><br>Number of librarians/total library staff (FTE)<br><br>Total staff per professional | | Number of clients served/library staff member |

# ESTABLISHING THE VALUE OF INFORMATION

Researchers have used a number of different approaches and techniques in attempting to establish the value of information and information services. It is possible to categorize or map these techniques, as shown in Figure 7.1. This mapping will allow us to determine the strengths and weaknesses of each approach and thus assess its potential utility for evaluating library and information services. Note that the map has two dimensions: situation-specificity (X-axis) and the context or focus of the analysis (Y-axis).

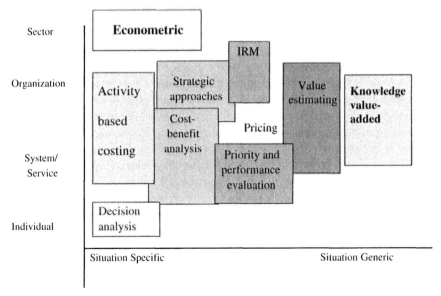

**Figure 7.1. Approaches to the Value of Information. Adapted from Douglas Badenoch, Christine Reid, Paul Burton, Forbes Gibb, and Charles Oppenheim. The Value of Information, in Mary Feeney and Maureen Grieves (Eds.). *The Value and Impact of Information.* London: Bowker Saur, 1994, 9-78.**

*Econometric approaches* use quantitative mathematical models of sectors of the economy, an industry, and so forth. Such an approach, though interesting, will have little utility in establishing the value of library and information services.

Similarly, there is a wealth of literature about the value of information and the impact information has as it is used by individuals and groups when they make decisions. Collectively this literature is called *decision analysis*. These methods are noted for information only.

Each of the other techniques shown in Figure 7.1 is examined in greater detail in the following sections to determine its potential applicability for assessing the value of a library and its information services.

## Pricing

Activity based costing (ABC) was discussed in Chapter 5. Cost accounting is an attempt to determine the amount of cost to be assigned to each unit of output. Even for smaller libraries, knowledge of the costs to provide various library services is an important first step to evaluating the library or a specific library service. Although ABC is more frequently used to identify the costs for a particular service, it is relatively easy to apply to all of a library's services.

For most libraries, the budget is considered to be a part of the overhead expenses for the running of the business or organization. The "invisible" nature of the library's budget is one of the major reasons why the management of some organizations does not understand or recognize the value of the library or information center. As an "overhead" expense, the first inclination among management is to reduce "nonessential" expenses in times of economic downturns.

An alternative to the "overhead" approach is to charge for services. There are several reasons to charge for an information service: (1) to generate income, (2) to ration demand, (3) to serve as an indirect measure of value, and (4) to convey a *perception* of value. Services are charged directly to the customer or department, which has the option of using other service providers that provide more value. Among libraries, the primary reason for pricing is to recover costs. The libraries in some nonprofit organizations charge for library services as a "benefit" of membership.

One of the appeals of pricing is that it helps the library recognize that there is competition in the information-providing arena. The Internet clearly provides a wealth of information, some of which is of high quality, but the Internet is only one of many competitive pressures facing a library or information center. Of course, turning to a nonlibrary resource requires considerably more effort and the expense of time on the part of an employee to find the information. The consideration of the value of time is addressed in Chapter 8.

Pricing can be cost-based, demand-based, or competition-based. Using activity based costing, the costs for all services are identified. These costs are then used to establish the price of a service. A demand-based pricing scheme will charge more for the more frequently used services and establishes lower pricing for the services that are seldom requested. The challenge with demand-based pricing is to ensure that sufficient "revenue" is raised during the year to cover the library's budget. Finally, competition-based pricing will establish prices that reflect the competitive environment. That is, if a for-profit search intermediary firm charges $X for its service, then this is the price the library would use to provide similar services.[1]

One of the major criticisms of pricing is that any price that is established is somewhat arbitrary and artificial. If the price is too high, then it will dampen demand and the need for the service will decline. If it is set too low, there may be too much demand for the service. Despite its potential appeal to serve as an indirect measure of value for the library, pricing does not reflect value and thus has no basis to be used as an indicator of the value of an information service.

## Strategic Approaches

Clark and Augustine suggest that it is possible that an information strategy can improve an organization's performance.[2] They examined four characteristics of information and information services: (1) accuracy, (2) timeliness, (3) reliability, and (4) relevance of the information provided. These information service characteristics were studied to determine what affect the characteristics had on an organization's operations, mid-level managers, and the strategy for the organization. Unfortunately, use of this approach almost requires the use of a consultant to gather and analyze the necessary data. The information characteristic having the greatest impact on the organization was the quality of information, as shown in Table 7.2.

**Table 7.2. Impact of Quality of Information on an Organization**

| Quality of Information | Operational | Managerial | Strategy |
|---|---|---|---|
| Low | Greatest effect on profitability | Less effect on profitability | Little impact |
| High | Little impact | Cannot overcome low quality information provided to operational areas | Little impact |

Using the information that they had collected, Clark and Augustine were able to determine the implications if the quality of information declined. Their analysis suggested that decreasing accuracy mainly affected profitability but had little impact on cost performance and efficiency. Decreased timeliness affected all aspects of a company's performance. Decreasing relevance had an impact on efficiency but little effect in other areas, whereas decreased reliability mainly affected profitability.

Work by Johnston[3] and Parker et al.[4] also suggests that using an information strategy can improve an organization's performance. These authors focus on the use of information technology, but by implication this same approach could be used to assess the information services provided by a library.

## Information Resources Management

Instead of considering information as an overhead expense, Horton and Marchand suggested that information is a resource that should be handled like any other resource within an organization.[5] Their approach, information resources management (IRM), is concerned with information assets, the content of information within the organization, and the people who handle the information. They indicate that information

Has fundamental value,

Has measurable characteristics,

Can be capitalized or expensed, and

As an input, can be transformed into useful outputs.

Horton and Marchand indicate that it is possible to *link corporate information resources and the organization's goals and objectives*. Thus, information used by management is only valuable if it *contributes* to better decisions or reduces risk for planned actions or activities. Using information resource management, information will either reduce costs or add value.

One of the best-known tools that may be used in information resource management analysis is the preparation of an information resource map,[6] which allows the organization to place its information resources into context so that they can be better exploited. The IRM process is primarily focused on an organizationwide perspective, although it can be applied to specific departments or activities. A number of firms have used IRM as a part of a larger business process reengineering program and found the methodology to be helpful. However, it should be noted that using IRM is a time-consuming and labor-intensive activity.

A variation of the IRM approach is to use a methodology called the "information audit" or the "strategic information audit."[7] The information audit typically uses a combination of a fairly comprehensive questionnaire and interviews with key individuals within an organization. Depending on the size of the organization, the volume of data that may need to analyzed can be significant. The purpose of the information audit is to

- Evaluate
    - The existing information delivery systems,
    - Current information needs,
    - Effectiveness of current information sources,
    - Effectiveness of technology to distribute information, and
    - Information uses and needs by functional areas; and
- Identify
    - Information management objectives of the organization,

-Information gaps and duplication of effort,

-New information sources, and

-Potential changes to existing systems (including the range of the library or information center services).

# Value Estimating

Another approach to determining the value of information and information services is to estimate those values. Value estimating can be done from the perspective of a single transaction, for example, visiting the library to obtain a document, as well as from the viewpoint of the organization as a whole.

Most firms focus on the issue of bandwidth, which allows for an increase in the speed with which information is transmitted and in the amount of information that can be processed. Such firms typically view information and information management from the perspective of cost. Other organizations choose to focus on the information value chain. Glazer[8] suggests that it is possible to aggregate three types of information-intensive transactions:

Transactions between the firm and its suppliers

Transactions within the firm

Transactions between the firm and its customers.

Glazer has developed an iterative methodology that allows people within an organization, especially a for-profit firm, to estimate the value of these information transactions. Given access to the appropriate information, (1) revenues from subsequent transactions are greater than they otherwise would be, (2) costs of subsequent transactions are lower than they otherwise would be, and (3) the information itself could be marketed. Armed with this perspective, managers are then asked to consider the value of information transactions using the following 12 categories:

Additional money from new customers

Additional money from current customers

Additional money from customized products to customers

Additional money from higher prices to customers

Additional money from sales promotions

Decreased advertising costs

Decreased direct mail costs

Decreased sales force costs

Decreased customer financing costs

Decreased customer service costs

Decreased order processing costs

Decreased inventory carrying costs

The second approach to estimating value, which focuses on a service transaction, is to ask the client of the library to provide an approximation of the value of the information or information service. In fact, this approach has been used by a number of researchers over the years as they seek to understand the implications of determining the value of library services.

## Cost-Benefit Analysis

The aim of any cost-benefit analysis is to identify the potential impact of a decision. At first glance, the prospect of preparing a cost-benefit analysis may be a bit overwhelming. The key is to concentrate on the level of effort in performing the analysis so that it is proportional to the importance of the decision. Obviously, the time and effort to prepare an analysis for a decision to spend $10,000 should be less than if a $1 million decision is the focus.

The analysis requires that each cost and benefit category be quantified. However, there is greater risk for the quantitative values assigned (estimated) for some categories. For example, some categories will have *hard impacts* (a cost for new computer software is obvious, and it is easy to determine the exact cost). *Soft impacts*, such as productivity gains, rely on uncontrollable factors, and thus there are greater risks to the estimates given to these categories. *Unquantifiable impacts*, such as improved customer satisfaction, are uncertain and difficult to ascribe value to and will have little or no impact in a cost-benefit analysis.

Despite the frequency with which it is used in almost every industry and government sector, cost-benefit analysis suffers from a lingering and troublesome problem. The costs are clearly understood and occur in a very specific time period, but the benefits, which are more difficult to quantify, are usually spread out over a longer period of time. The costs are typically identified using the ABC methodology discussed earlier.

Five possible methods are available to prepare a cost-benefit analysis, and the different approaches can yield different results.[9] The choice of the most appropriate cost-benefit analysis method depends on the situation:

1. **Maximize benefits for a given cost**. If the library only has $10,000 to spend on a project or activity, then this first method is appropriate.

2. **Minimize costs for a given level of benefits**. If the library knows exactly the benefits it wishes to achieve and is not interested in additional benefits, even if they are available and cost more, then this method of analysis is appropriate.

3. **Maximize the ratio of benefits over costs.** Often the alternatives present a wide range of costs and a correspondingly wide range of benefits. In this case, this method of analysis should be used. Results of this type of analysis are often expressed as a ratio of benefits to costs, for example, $16 worth of benefits for every $1 of costs or 16:1.

4. **Maximize the net benefits** (present value of benefits over present value of costs). This method recognizes that costs are likely to be incurred first and that benefits often have different starting points or "benefit streams." A present value analysis recognizes that a dollar today is worth more than a dollar received at some point in the future.

5. **Maximize the internal rate of return** when preparing a return on investment (ROI) analysis. Typically this method is done in the for-profit sector.

The approach, "Maximize benefits while costs are minimized," is a contradiction in terms and cannot be accomplished.

In addition to using the cost-benefit analysis for specific projects, the methodology has been applied to identifying the return on investment or ROI for two very similar departments within an organization: information technology and the library. Aside from the time it can take to prepare a comprehensive cost-benefit analysis for library information services, the real usefulness will be the way librarians, library clients, and organizational managers gain a shared understanding of the value of the library and its information services.

Preparing the cost-benefit analysis can be made easier if the following suggestions are considered:

- Clearly, the most challenging task in any cost-benefit analysis is how to estimate the benefit in quantifiable terms: dollars and cents or, as some cynics have noted, "dollars and sense." The benefit should not be included in the cost-benefit analysis if it can't be quantified.

- Be conservative in estimating benefits and liberal in assessing costs. To obtain better estimates, the following steps are suggested:

  1. Identify and quantify benefits *first*.

  2. Identify each benefit that will be achieved as a result of the project or service. Benefits are defined as "the consequence of an action, that protects, aids, improves, or promotes the well-being of an individual or organization. Benefits take the form of cost savings, cost avoidance, improved operational performance, better allocation of resources, and 'intangibles,' e.g., better understanding of a particular situation."[10]

  3. Identify and calculate costs for each alternative. Ensure that all cost components are included in the analysis.[11]

Following these suggestions will help prevent estimating benefits so that they almost always exceed costs. It is not too often that the phrase "runaway benefits or benefit overruns" is heard to describe the status of a project.[12]

Other costs and factors may also be a part of the analysis, including the following:

1. **Transition costs.** Are there any one-time costs associated with moving from one system to another? Training costs?

2. **Complexity costs.** Investing in new technologies means that the organization needs to support additional technologies and standards. What will happen to the support costs for these new technologies?

3. **Technical risk.** How likely is it that things can go wrong? What would be the impact? Are there any contingency plans? In some organizations, this is referred to as scenario planning.

4. **Flexibility value.** Investing in infrastructure or a new technology may enhance or impede future projects. Would a new technology have an impact on the speed of software development or the implementation process? Would a new system give the library the flexibility to provide personalized services?

5. **Marketplace factors.** Will the technology vendor be around for a while? Does the vendor have a proven track record? Is the vendor delivering "best in class" technology?

Normally, a brief report documenting the analysis and the recommended approach is prepared. Within the library community, the cost-benefit method of comparing the ratio of benefits to costs is normally used.

## Depreciation

When a purchased asset will be used over a number of years, its cost is spread over its useful life through an accounting process called depreciation. The simplest method of depreciation is to charge an equal amount for each year of its life (this method is called straight-line depreciation). Typically assets more than a certain amount are depreciated, for example, equipment and servers. Note that depreciation is an accounting tool and does not affect the expenditure of funds to pay for the asset. To establish the appropriate depreciation period, it is necessary to determine the "relevant life" of the average item in the collection. This will vary by type of library. There are, not surprisingly, some advantages and disadvantages to various depreciation methods:

- The "straight-line" method is not recommended because it does not reflect the half-life usage of a collection. For example, the depreciation period for the library's collection is 20 years, so each year the collection asset is depreciated by 5 percent.

- The "sum-of-the-years digits" method is recommended because it models the half-life usage pattern of a collection. For example, the depreciation period is 10 years, so the "sum-of-the-years digits" is $10 + 9 + 8 + 7 + \ldots = 55$. So the first year, the collection is depreciated 18 percent (10/55).

- An alternative is to use the "declining balance or reducing balance method," which doubles the straight-line value. For example, the depreciation period is 20 years, so each year the collection asset is depreciated by 10 percent, not 5 percent. Thus, if there were no additions to the library's collection, it would be worthless (from a depreciation stand point) after 10 years.

When an asset is purchased, its useful life is recorded along with its cost. Depreciation is recorded in an account called *accumulated depreciation*. The cost minus the accumulated depreciation is its *book value*. Some assets are assumed to have no value at the end of their useful life, whereas other assets will have *residual* or *salvage value*.

In some organizations the library's collection is never depreciated; in others the collection is an important asset and thus should be valued.[13] Two types of collections can be identified:

- **Current use collection:** A collection in the day-to-day operations of a library. Individual items in the collection show a pattern of declining use, obsolescence, or physically wearing out.[14]

- **Permanent retained collection:** A collection that has cultural, aesthetic, or historical value, which is worth preserving, for example, the collections of archives or cultural collections. Depreciation of the collection, as an asset, should *never* be done.

What is the value of the collection to the organization? What would it cost to replace the services the organization obtains from the collection? This is known as the *deprival value* of the collection.

Following are two approaches to establishing the initial value of the collection:

- **Actual cost of each item.** Use actual cost; depreciate the item based on age on an item-by-item basis.

- **Estimated value.** Use an average of the cost of each item and depreciate for the average age of the collection.

After the initial value is established, the collection value should be updated annually based on the actual costs of items added and withdrawn from the collection.

The question then arises, should a library depreciate its collection? Probably not, since the value of the asset is being "refreshed" each year through the addition of new materials to the collection while, at the same time, some materials are being withdrawn from the collection since they no longer have any "value."

A library can, however, use depreciation as a method to assess the adequacy of the library's annual materials collection budget:

- If the annual collection materials budget *equals* the depreciated value, then the materials acquisitions budget is adequate.

- If the annual collection materials budget is *greater* than the depreciated value, then the collection asset is increasing in value and the library is blessed.

- If the annual collection materials budget is *less* than the depreciated value, then the collection asset is declining in value. This should be a red flag!

Often for insurance purposes a library will track the value of its collection using a replacement cost as a basis for valuation rather than a depreciated value. The reason for this is that if all or a portion of the collection is damaged or destroyed, the costs to replace the collection may be more than the original purchase price. For insurance purposes, determining the percent of the collection out on loan at the time of disaster may reduce the value of the collection.

## Knowledge Value-Added Approach

Kanevsky and Housel developed the knowledge value-added methodology as a tool to assist businesses in the process of business reengineering.[15] This tool focuses on the organization as a whole or at least on a significant portion of the business. The basic tenet of the knowledge value-added process is to identify surrogate measures for determining how much an intangible asset, namely knowledge, is embedded in each process that leads to a specific product or service. Some have suggested that knowledge value-added provides a clearer picture of how knowledge is used to create products and services than ABC.[16]

Portugal has provided a step-by-step approach, including use of an example of a company involved in developing a new drug, of the knowledge value-added process, in *Valuating Information Intangibles*.[17] Once all of the calculations have been made it is possible to calculate a return on knowledge (ROK)—the ratio of revenue yield to expenses for each subprocess. One of the subprocesses in Portugal's example was library service. The return on knowledge for this example was 54:1; that is, the library provided a return of $54 of intangible value for every dollar invested in the library service.

Since the primary focus of the knowledge value-added process is at the organizational level, most libraries will find difficulty in applying this methodology to the evaluation of library services.

## Summary of Evaluation Techniques

Some of the evaluation methodologies are clearly more applicable for the purpose of evaluating and measuring the outcomes or impacts of the library on the larger organization. These evaluation techniques are summarized in Table 7.3. The bottom line for a library is to identify its evaluation needs and then pick one or more evaluation methodologies that will work best.

### Table 7.3. Summary of Evaluation Methodologies

| Method | Approach | Focus | Impact on Library | Impact on Organization |
|---|---|---|---|---|
| | | | | |
| Activity based costing | Analysis | Library | Moderate | Limited |
| Pricing | Analysis | Library | Limited | Limited |
| Strategic approaches | Analysis/Survey | Org | Limited | Moderate |
| Information resource management | Analysis/Survey | Org | Limited | Moderate |
| Value estimating | Survey | Org | Significant | Moderate |
| PAPE | Survey | Org | Significant | Significant |
| Cost-benefit analysis | Survey/Analysis | Org | Significant | Moderate |
| Knowledge value-added | Analysis | Org | Limited | Moderate |

Org = Organization

Most libraries will use two to three of these techniques. More than likely the techniques of highest potential value will be PAPE, ABC (both discussed in Chapter 5), and a value estimating survey used in conjunction with a cost-benefit analysis.

## DETERMINING THE IMPACT OF A LIBRARY

Determining an effective strategy for evaluating library services involves the following problems:

- The "bottom line" is too far away. The provision of a library service, at one point in time, has no clear link to the financial well-being of the larger organization, typically assessed at a later point in time.

- The managers or executives of the larger organization are too far away, given their day-to-day responsibilities, to even consider or be interested in evaluating the library.

- Library staff are too involved in providing library services and have difficulty in seeing the "big picture."

Considering these problems, it would seem that the clients of the library would be best able make an assessment of the contribution of the library to the larger organization.

Saracevic and Kantor developed a framework and taxonomy for establishing the value that may arise from using library and information services based on the vocabulary of users in responding to a questionnaire.[18] They suggest that a client has three potential reasons to use a library or information service: (1) to work on a task or project, (2) for personal reasons, or (3) to get an object or information or perform an activity. They also state that when a client interacts with a library service, three areas of interaction should be considered:

- **Resources**. From the client's perspective, there are three issues that might be considered in this area:

  –*Availability*. This traditional evaluation measure attempts to assess whether the library has the given resource, item, or service desired by the client.

  –*Accessibility*. This measure focuses on the ease with which the service can be accessed. Is a visit to the library required, for example?

  –*Quality*. This measure assesses the degree to which a service or resource is accurate, current, timely, and complete.

- **Use of resources, services**. In examining this area, the library could ask its clients to assess five potential measures:

  –The degree of *convenience* in using the resource or service.

  –*Ease of use*. How difficult is it to use a resource or library service?

  –What *frustration*, if any, results from using the resource or library service?

  –How *successful* is the client in using a library service or resource?

  –How much *effort* is required to move from one service to another? An example is performing a search to identify citations and then retrieving the desired journal articles or other resources.

- **Operations and environment**. There are four categories in which clients can be asked to rate the library and its services in this area:

  - How reasonable and clear are the library's *policies and procedures*? Do they facilitate access to the library's services or act as impediments?

  - Are the *facilities* of adequate size? Do the physical layout and organization of the library resources facilitate access to the resources and services?

  - Are library *staff members* helpful, efficient, and knowledgeable? Is there a clear understanding of the goals and objectives of the organization and a desire by library staff to offer a quality service?

  - Is the equipment reliable and easy to use? Are user instructions or guides readily available?

But most important, Saracevic and Kantor focused on the results, outcomes, or impact that a library or information service has on the organization. Given a reason to use the library, and having had an interaction with one or more library services, what is the effect? They grouped this impact into six categories:

- **Cognitive results**. Use of the library may have an impact on the mind of the client. The intent of this category is to ask the question, "What was learned?" Thus, the client may have

  - Refreshed memory of detail or facts;

  - Substantiated or reinforced knowledge or belief;

  - Provided new knowledge;

  - A change in viewpoint, outlook, or perspective;

  - Ideas with a slightly different or tangential perspective (serendipity); or

  - No ideas.

- **Affective results**. Use of the library or its services may influence or have an emotional impact on the client. The client may experience

  - A sense of accomplishment, success, or satisfaction;

  - A sense of confidence, reliability, and trust;

  - A sense of comfort, happiness, and good feelings;

  - A sense of failure; or

  - A sense of frustration.

- **Meeting expectations**. When using the library or an information service, clients may

    −Be getting what they needed, sought, or expected;

    −Be getting too much;

    −Be getting nothing.

    −Have confidence in what they have received;

    −Receive more than they expected; or

    −Seek substitute sources or action if what they received did not meet expectations.

- **Accomplishments** in relation to tasks. As a result of using the library, the client may be

    −Able to make better informed decisions;

    −Achieve a higher quality performance;

    −Able to point to a course of action;

    −Proceeding to the next step;

    −Discovering people and/or other sources of information; or

    −Improving a policy, procedure, and plan.

- **Time aspects**. Some of the real value for the client of a library is the fact that the information provided might lead to the saving of time in several possible ways. The client may

    −Save time as a result of using the service,

    −Waste time as a result of using the service,

    −Need to wait for service,

    −Experience a service that ranges from slow to fast, or

    −Need time to understand how to use a service or resource.

- **Money aspects**. Using the library or information service may, in some cases, clearly result in saving money or generating new revenues. The client may be able to provide an

    −Estimate of the dollar value of results obtained from a service or information received,

    −Estimate of the amount of money saved due to the use of the service,

    −Estimate of the cost in using the service,

    −Estimate of what may be spent on a substitute service, or

    −Estimate of value (in dollars) lost where the service was not available or use was not successful.

Saracevic and Kantor suggest that it is possible to create a survey instrument that can be used to assess the outcome or impact of the library and its information services on the clients of the library. Unfortunately, the model developed by Saracevic and Kantor, although comprehensive, is long and difficult to replicate. It should be noted that the first three results (cognitive, affective, and expectations) would normally translate in some way to having an impact on the latter three outcomes (accomplishments, time, and money). If there is no link between a cognitive aspect, for example, refreshing an individual's memory about a fact, and a time or money outcome, then that particular information transaction is not directly affecting the organization and would not be "counted" as a measurable outcome.

## SUMMARY

This chapter has demonstrated that there are a variety of ways to attempt to determine the value of a library and the services that it provides. A majority of special libraries will be interested in assessing the value of the library by asking customers to estimate the real impact of the library in terms of accomplishments, time savings, and money savings. Once this information has been gathered, a library can then prepare a cost-benefit analysis to communicate to its various stakeholders the true "value" of the library to the larger organization. This information will assist the librarian in demonstrating that the library is not a cost center but rather a "value center" that provides to the organization a real return on its investment.

## NOTES

1. Yvette Tilson. Income Generation and Pricing in Libraries. *Library Management*, 15 (2), 1994, 5–17.

2. T. D. Clark and F. K. Augustine. Using System Dynamics to Measure the Value of Information to a Business Firm. *Systems Dynamics Review*, 8, 1990, 149–73.

3. H. R. Johnston. Developing Capabilities to Use Information Strategically. *MIS Quarterly*, March 1988, 36–48.

4. Marilyn M. Parker and H. Edgar Trainor with Robert J. Benson. *Information Strategy and Economics*. London: Prentice-Hall, 1989.

5. D. Marchand and F. W. Horton. *InfoTrends: Profiting from Your Information Resources*. New York: John Wiley, 1986.

6. Cornelius F. Burk and Forest W. Horton. *Infomap: A Complete Guide to Discovering Corporate Information Sources*. New York: John Wiley, 1991.

7. *The Information Audit: An SLA Information Kit*. Washington, DC: The Special Libraries Association, 1995.

8. R. Glazer. Measuring the Value of Information: The Information-Intensive Organization. *IBM Systems Journal*, 32 (1), 1993, 99–110.

9. John L. King and Edward L. Schrems. Cost-Benefit Analysis of Information Systems Development and Operation." *Computing Surveys*, 10 (1), March 1978, 22–34. For a review of the economics involved in creating a cost-benefit analysis, see Bruce R. Kingma. *The Economics of Information: A Guide to Economic and Cost-Benefit Analysis for Information Professionals*. Englewood, CO: Libraries Unlimited, 2001.

10. Ibid.

11. For a further elaboration of cost-benefit analysis, see Joseph R. Matthews. *Internet Outsourcing Using an Application Service Provider: A How-to-Do-It Manual for Librarians*. New York: Neal-Schuman, 2001.

12. John L. King and Kenneth L. Kraemer. Cost as a Social Impact of Information Technology, in N. L. Moss (Ed.). *Telecommunication and Productivity*. Reading, MA: Addison-Wesley, 1981.

13. Jennifer Cram. Not an Inexhaustible Resource: Valuation and Depreciation of Library Collections. *Australian Library Journal*, 46 (4), 1997, 376–85. Available at http://alia.org/~jcram/not_inexhaustible.html (accessed July9, 2002).

14. Edward Marman. A Method for Establishing a Depreciated Monetary Value for a Print Collection. *Library Administration & Management*, 9 (2), 1995, 94–98; and Murray S. Martin. What Is Your Library Worth? *Technicalities*, 15 (9), 1995, 4–5.

15. Valery Kanevsky and Tom Housel. *The Learning-Knowledge-Value Cycle: Tracking the Velocity of Change in Knowledge to Value*. Available at http://www.businessprcessaudits.com/vluecycle.htm (accessed July 9, 2002).

16. Victoria Nomuura and Kimberly O'Connor. *Knowledge Value Added and Activity Based Costing: A Comparison of Re-engineering Methodologies*. Available at http://www.businessprcessaudits.com (accessed July 9, 2002).

17. Frank H. Portugal. *Valuating Information Intangibles: Measuring the Bottom Line Contribution of Librarians and Information Professionals*. Washington, DC: Special Libraries Association, 2000.

18. Tefko Saracevic and Paul B. Kantor. Studying the Value of Library and Information Services. Part I. Establishing a Theoretical Framework. *Journal of the American Society of Information Science*, 48 (6), 1997, 527–42; Tefko Saracevic and Paul B. Kantor. Studying the Value of Library and Information Services. Part II. Methodology and Taxonomy. *Journal of the American Society of Information Science*, 48 (6), 1997, 543–63.

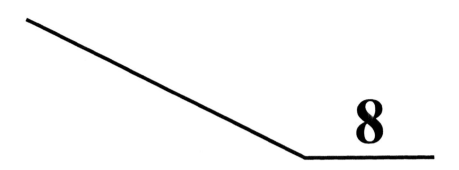

# 8

# Outcomes in Special Libraries

*Everybody gets so much information all day long that
they lose their common sense.*

—Gertrude Stein

Using one or more of the approaches identified in Chapter 7, a number of
studies have focused on ways to determine the value of the library and the information services it provides. The outcome or impact the special library and its information services have on the larger organization are summarized here using
three major outcome categories: accomplishments, time, and money.

## ACCOMPLISHMENTS

Accomplishments can be viewed as the category of outcome or impact that
is not related to time or money impacts. Further, accomplishments can be
viewed both from a positive perspective and as avoiding negative consequences, as articulated most clearly by Joanne Marshall in some of her studies.
For example, Marshall suggests that information services can assist the organization by avoiding

Poor business decisions,

Conflict within the institution, and

Conflict with another institution.[1]

A case in point illustrates the consequences of a poor decision-making process when incomplete information about a particular topic becomes one of the components of a decision. A medical researcher at John Hopkins University conducted an online search about the potential side effects of a particular chemical compound, which was being considered for testing on humans.[2] The researcher did not conduct a thorough search of the published paper-based literature, found in the library, which preceded the start of the online database. Based on the search results, the trial for human testing commenced, and one of the volunteers subsequently died. For a period of time, all medical trials at John Hopkins University were stopped. Now, researchers must collaborate with a librarian and pharmacist to ensure that a search of medical literature is comprehensive and thorough.[3]

# TIME ASPECTS

One of the principal values of a library and its information services is that they significantly improve the productivity of the clients of the library and thus the efficiency of the larger organization. The main reason this is so is that the cost of an information professional's time continues to be less than that of other professionals (for example, doctors, engineers, lawyers, and senior managers). This is compounded by the fact that an information professional is trained and is thus much more efficient in finding information resources, conducting online searches, and so forth. Thus, it is the combination of the cost differential plus more efficient searching that makes these more expensive professionals more productive and ultimately leads to a cost savings for the organization.

Helen Manning, the librarian at Texas Instruments, surveyed library users and asked them to identify the impact of library services on their jobs, the number of hours saved as a result of using library services, and the number of hours saved by the librarian.[4] Despite a low response rate to the survey, Manning calculated that the total savings to Texas Instruments from the library was $959,000. Given the operating budget of $186,000, the return on investment was 515 percent, or a benefit/cost ratio of 5.15:1.

In a wide range of studies, Griffiths and King have focused on the apparent value of information services. That is, they focused on the time and effort that would be required by an individual to identify, locate, order, receive, and use the needed information compared to the time required (and thus, the cost) if these tasks were performed by a library.[5] The typical special library spends a range of $400 to $1,000 per year per professional employee (in 1993 dollars). If the library was eliminated and other sources of information were used to provide the equivalent information, the organization would spend considerably more than it does for a library. (Griffiths and King report a 3:1 return on investment.) Table 8.1 compares the cost of obtaining documents from the library and outside the organization (per professional staff member per year). Griffiths and King argue that the $2,680 of savings per professional employee per year more than offsets the $800 or so that would be spent on a library.

## Table 8.1. Cost Comparison of Information Retrieval

| With a Library | Costs* | No Library | Costs* |
|---|---|---|---|
| Library subscription cost | $ 515 | | |
| Library | 95 | Getting document | $3,290 |
| Professionals' finding time | 840 | Professionals' finding time | 840 |
| Professionals' reading time | 4,100 | Professionals' reading time | 4,100 |
| Total | $5,550 | Total | $8,230 |

*1973 dollars

The net result of these studies is that libraries provide better information, faster and less expensively than is possible with other alternatives. By providing timely, quality information services that meet the needs of the professionals within an organization, the library helps to increase the quality, timeliness, and productivity of these individuals and ultimately enhances the performance of the larger organization.

Griffiths and King report that professionals spend a considerable amount of time reading journal articles, books, internal reports, and other documents (professionals average 198 readings per year). The professionals do spend a considerable amount of time acquiring and reading documents, even those provided by the library (an average of 288 hours per year; see Figure 8.1). This reading, in turn, leads these professionals to avoid having to do certain work, modifying their existing work, or stopping an unproductive line of work.

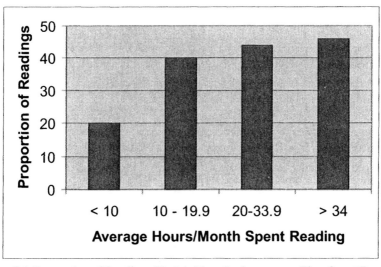

Figure 8.1. Proportion of Readings That Achieve Savings versus Time Spent Reading

These same professionals have also estimated the value of receiving information from the library as opposed to their acquiring the documents themselves. On average, the return on investment ranged from 7.8:1 to 14.2:1. (These data were published in 1993, so libraries citing this and other information in the report should make adjustments for inflation.)

Harris and Marshall prepared a cost-benefit analysis that examined a library's current awareness bulletin using the approach to identify the value of time (and hence money) saved by reading the bulletin as compared to needing to spend the time and energy to seek the information from other sources. They found a benefit to cost ratio of 9:1.[6] Readers of the current awareness bulletin felt that they saved time and also were introduced to new ways of doing things, avoided duplication of effort, and increased their individual productivity. In addition to the positive impact of improving a person's productivity, the flip side also exists, as noted by Marshall.[7] Without the appropriate information, a person can experience loss (waste) of his or her own time or loss of another person's time.

Professional employees spend an average of 9.5 hours per week obtaining, reviewing, and analyzing information.[8] This is roughly one-quarter of the time they spend working each week and represents a significant expenditure of their time at the workplace. This expenditure of time or attention is the currency of exchange for information. This scarcity of attention relative to the abundant amount of available information provides for an "attentional economy," according to Thorngate. He has suggested six principles that arise from an attentional economy (see Table 8.2).

## Table 8.2. Six Principles of an Attentional Economy

| | |
|---|---|
| Fixed attentional assets | Attention is a finite and a nonrenewable resource. |
| Singular attentional investments | Attention can, in general, be invested in only one activity at a time. |
| Diminishing attentional returns | The more attention we continuously invest in one thing, the less it is likely to continue holding our attention. |
| Expected attentional revenues | Attentional investments are generally made in expectation of future rewards. |
| Exploratory attentional expenses | Whenever we search for and choose attentional investments, the acts of searching and choosing themselves require attentional investments. |
| Balanced attentional budgets | Attention paid should equal attention received. |

*Source:* **Developed from information contained in Warren Thorngate. On Paying Attention, in William J. Baker, Leendert P. Mos, Hans V. Rappard, and Henderikus J. Stam (Eds.).** *Recent Trends in Theoretical Psychology.* **New York: Springer-Verlag, 1987, 247–63.**

The constantly increasing volume of information means that any criteria developed to separate the informational wheat from the chaff will be problematic. As we seek information we are likely to make two kinds of errors: of commission (reading something that has little or no value) and of omission (overlooking something we shouldn't). Sampling an ever-decreasing proportion of worthwhile articles, reports, and so forth means that we are ever more likely to overlook that which would provide insight, solve a problem, suggest a new direction for research, and so forth.

# COST ASPECTS

Two approaches to identifying the cost aspects of the library and its information services can be used. These include ascertaining the relative value and the consequential value of an information service.

The *relative value* approach seeks to identify the cost to use alternative sources of information compared to the nominal cost of providing the library service. According to Griffiths and King, on average, an organization without a library will spend more than three times as much per year per professional to obtain information services as an organization with a library (in 1993 dollars):

> Without library     $5,010
> With library        $1,700[9]

Using the information obtained from these various surveys, Griffiths and King were able to establish the value for a particular library service if the library performed the service on behalf of a client (see Table 8.3, page 94). Multiplying the value of a service, for example, online database searching times the number of times this service is performed each year, will result in a total value for the service ($272.00 x 13,500 searches performed each year provides a total value of $3,672,000). Using this information, some libraries have combined these estimated values with the volume of activity for each service and then calculated the total estimated value for all library services (see Table 8.4, page 95, for an example of calculations using this approach).

This estimated value approach is based on the assumption that each service transaction results in true "savings" for an organization, but clearly this is not always the case. Yet this approach can be an effective starting point that the library director can use when discussing the value of the library with the management team of the organization.

### Table 8.3. Library Services and Their Estimated Value

| Library Service and Estimated Value* | Number of Library Services | Total Value of Library Service |
|---|---|---|
| Online literature database searching (excluding Internet) Valued at $ 272.00 per search | | |
| Interlibrary loans borrowed for a client Valued at $ 138.00 per loan | | |
| Journals routed to clients Valued at $ 57.31 per journal routed | | |
| Item circulated to a client from the collection Valued at $51.49 per item loaned | | |
| Reference questions answered for clients (Answers require less than 10 minutes of research) Valued at $ 7.50 per question | | |
| Reference questions answered for clients (Answers require more than 10 minutes of research) Valued at $ 45.00 per question | | |
| Item ordered specifically for a client Valued at $ 30.57 per item | | |
| Article reprints purchased for clients Valued at $ 138.00 per article | | |
| Photocopies made for clients Valued at $ 29.27 per article | | |
| Use of online databases by the client Valued at $ 16.67 per search session | | |
| Use of online catalog by client Valued at $ 17.00 per client | | |
| Current awareness service used by client Valued at $ 56.90 per item requested | | |
| Total Value for Library Services | | |

* **Values derived from Jose-Marie Griffiths and Donald W. King. *Special Libraries: Increasing the Information Edge*. Washington, DC: Special Libraries Association, 1993.**

## Table 8.4. Estimated Value of Library Services

| Library Service and Estimated Value* | Number of Library Services | Total Value of Library Service |
|---|---|---|
| Online literature database searching (excluding Internet) Valued at $ 272.00 per search | 13,500 searches | $ 3,672,000 |
| Interlibrary loans borrowed for a client Valued at $ 138.00 per loan | 9,100 | 1,225,800 |
| Journals routed to clients Valued at $ 57.31 per journal routed | 58,400 | 3,346,904 |
| Item circulated to a client from the collection Valued at $51.49 per item loaned | 43,300 | 2,229,517 |
| Reference questions answered for clients (Answers require less than 10 minutes of research) Valued at $ 7.50 per question | 55,400 | 415,500 |
| Reference questions answered for clients (Answers require more than 10 minutes of research) Valued at $ 45.00 per question | 22,700 | 1,021,500 |
| Item ordered specifically for a client Valued at $ 30.57 per item | 8,800 | 269,016 |
| Article reprints purchased for clients Valued at $ 138.00 per article | 3,300 | 455,400 |
| Photocopies made for clients Valued at $ 29.27 per article | 13,700 | 400,999 |
| Use of online databases by the client Valued at $ 16.67 per search session | 12,000 | 200,040 |
| Use of online catalog by client Valued at $ 17.00 per client | 12,000 | 204,000 |
| Current awareness service used by client Valued at $ 56.90 per item requested | 15,800 | 899,020 |
| Total Value for Library Services | | $ 14,339,696 |

* Values derived from Jose-Marie Griffiths and Donald W. King. *Special Libraries: Increasing the Information Edge.* Washington, DC: Special Libraries Association, 1993.

The second approach is to identify the *consequential value* of using the library and its information services. The approach here is to ask the library client (user) what the financial impact of each information service transaction (or for a sample of transactions) is. The decision of whether to use a sample would be based on the volume of activity within the library (a sample size of several hundred would be desirable). The trade-off involves asking the client at the end of each information transaction or only for the sample (the possible nuisance factor declines using a sample). An example of the form that can be used to ask clients to place a financial value on the information service is shown in Figure 8.2.

---

Name: _____ Position: _____

How much time would you estimate you saved by having the library obtain the information rather than you having to do it yourself? _____hours

What monetary value (generate new revenue/save money) can you place on having the information?   $_____

How will having the information contribute to achieving your department's or project's goals? _____
_____

*Note:* The position (alternatively the personnel classification) will identify the likely annual salary for the individual, which is necessary to determine the value of this person's time.

---

**Figure 8.2. Assessment of Library Services. From Jennifer Cram. Moving from Cost Centre to Profitable Investment: Managing the Perception of a Library's Worth. *Australasian Public Libraries and Information Services*, 8 (3), 1995, 107–13. Reprinted with permission.**

Some libraries wait about a week and then contact by telephone the individual who responded to the survey. The survey questions are repeated. In some cases, individuals are able to think of some additional benefits that will accrue through the use of the information service that they have overlooked initially. Alternatively, the data about the utility of the library or information center could be obtained using an annual survey (see Appendix C). The disadvantage of the annual survey is that it relies on customers to make estimates about the impact of the library during the previous year, and these estimates are likely to be on the conservative side.

Once the data about the financial impact have been gathered, a cost-benefit analysis can be prepared. On the one hand the benefits from using the library have been identified by the clients (quantifying the benefits). On the other hand, the costs for providing library services are fairly well known (using the library's budget and preparing an ABC analysis to identify the indirect and overhead costs to the organization).[10] The preparation of the cost-benefit analysis allows the library to prepare an estimate of the library's ROI.

Portugal suggests that there are two variations that can be followed when the cost-benefit analysis is prepared. The first approach tallies all of the financial benefits in the form of savings and reports this as shown in Table 8.5 (Option A). The second approach tallies all of the financial benefits in the form of savings and also includes estimates of losses that may have arisen as the result of using the information service (Table 8.5, Option B).

### Table 8.5. Cost-Benefit Analysis Options

| Activity | Option A *Savings $ in Millions* | Option B *Savings (Loss) $ in Millions* |
|---|---|---|
| Key to competitive information | 3.4 | 3.4 |
| Eliminate some patents | 1.2 | 1.2 |
| Key report recovered | .2 | .2 |
| Technical references alter product | 2.2 | 2.2 |
| Search information unused | — | (2.3) |
| | | |
| Total | 7.0 | 4.7 |

*Note:* Library budget is $250,000.

Depending on which option is chosen, the cost-benefit ratio will range from 28:1 to 18.8:1 (assuming a library operating budget of $250,000). Clearly, either option demonstrates that the library is providing real dividends as the result of its services and thus the library should not be considered an overhead expense.

Griffiths and King studied the savings that resulted from the application of the information attained in reading. They conducted research across three industries and found that benefits ranged from 26:1 (a 2,600 percent return) to 17:1 (a 1,700 percent return).

Other studies report similar results. In her analysis of document delivery studies, Estabrook found that there was a range of benefits that varied from $2 to $48 saved for every $1 spent.[11] In an earlier review of cost-benefit studies, Manning reported a ratio of savings to cost of about 5 to 1.[12] And Koenig, in an article that reviewed the cost-benefit methodologies, identified a number of studies that resulted in a range of benefits to cost of 2.5:1 to 26:1. Koenig suggested that a conservative approach that would summarize the value ratio should be 2:1.[13]

Freeing up a professional's time to identify and obtain relevant information can have a considerable beneficial impact on an organization. One survey of nine corporations found that the professionals were able to quantify the value of information received, the value of which ranged from $2,500 to $15,000 per document used.[14]

In addition to saving money, the information provided by the library may spur additional revenues (via revenues from existing products and services to existing customers and/or attracting and retaining new customers), lead to the development of new products and services, shorten the product/service development life cycle, and so forth.

One of the easiest traps for librarians to fall into is to rely on statements about intangible benefits and not think clearly about how the intangible benefit actually translates into an economic benefit. For example, a survey of physicians indicated that information provided by their hospital or medical libraries led to several intangible benefits, as shown in Figure 8.3.

---

Assist in preventing patient deaths
Avoid surgery
Avoid additional tests and/or procedures
Reduced length of hospital stay
Avoid hospital admission
Changed the planned medical care for the patient
Changed the advice provided to patients
Changed patient diagnosis
Changed the medical tests requested
Changed prescriptions for medications

---

**Figure 8.3. Medical Intangible Benefits. From Judy Quinn and Michael Rogers. Study Shows Hospital Library Saves Lives. *Library Journal*, 116 (17), October 15, 1991, 12. Copyright 1991 Reed Business Information, a division of Reed Elsevier Inc. All rights reserved. Reprinted by permission of *Library Journal.***

Yet some of these "intangible" benefits have a direct connection to lowering costs (reduced length of hospital stay, not checking into the hospital in the first place). And although doctors are certainly not able to establish the value of human life, lawyers and juries deal with this topic more frequently than we would wish to acknowledge and are able to establish an economic value for the "worth of an individual's life."

In a similar healthcare arena, Marshall[15] asked respondents to a questionnaire to identify the value of information in three areas: quality of information, cognitive value, and value for decision making. She reported that physicians found that information provided by hospital librarians contributed to changes in

Diagnosis,

Choice of medical tests,

Choice of treatment,

Reduced length of hospital stay, and

Avoiding adverse medical consequences.

In the corporate banking environment, Marshall found that information provided by the librarian led to a combination of intangible and tangible benefits, including

The ability to proceed to the next step of a project or task,

Deciding on a course of action,

Exploiting new business opportunities,

Saving time, and

Avoiding loss of funds.[16]

In the government sector, Marshall found that use of information services led to some of the benefits noted above and also contributed to the

Ability to improve or approve a procedure, plan, or policy;

Ability to meet a deadline or cope with an unexpected emergency; and

Ability to prevent conflict within the government agency and outside the agency with another jurisdiction.[17]

Koenig reports that in the literature there is a link between the productivity of an organization and the variety and quality of information contacts.[18] He compared the information environment of the more-productive companies with the less-productive and found that the more-productive were characterized by

Greater openness to information from outside the company,

Less concern about protecting proprietary information,

Investing more in the development of information systems,

Greater end-user use of information systems; more encouragement of browsing and serendipity,

Greater technical and subject sophistication of library staff members, and

Unobtrusive R&D managerial structures.

Another approach would be to develop a measure of the output of the professionals associated with the organization. This would be an indirect measure of the impact of the library on the organization. Among the metrics that might be included in such a measure are

The number of publications (sorted by articles published in peer-review journals, articles in other journals, books, internal technical reports, and so forth),

The number of patents, and

Awards received from professional associations and societies.

# SALES TO THIRD PARTIES

Some organizations, for example associations, provide access to collections and library services as a perk to their members or other third parties. In some cases, the individuals who avail themselves of these services are expected to pay. Thus, the library is expected to generate revenues for the larger organization.

# SUMMARY

For the special library, there is compelling evidence that libraries provide information services that have real value to the larger organization. This value may be in the form of accomplishments, time savings, and financial impacts—both financial savings and increased revenues. A number of libraries have been participants in studies or have gathered the data themselves to calculate a cost-benefit analysis. Although the range of benefits to cost that result from library and information center services can be substantial, the positive financial impacts for the larger organization are significant and should not be ignored.

In some organizational cultures, the library director would be better served by considering the return on investment rather than the cost-benefit ratio. For example, for-profit companies will more than likely be interested in a ROI calculation, whereas nonprofit organizations and governmental agencies would be more interested in a cost-benefit ratio.

# NOTES

1. Joanne Gard Marshall. *The Impact of the Special Library on Corporate Decision-Making*. Washington, DC: Special Libraries Association, 1993.

2. Collaboration with Librarian Required in Hopkins' Report. *Corporate Library Update*, 10 (13), September 15, 2001, 1. All documents related to the report can be found at www.Hopkins-medicine.org.

3. For more information about the revised research procedures, visit http://www.hopkinsmedicine.org/press/2001/august/actionplan.htm (accessed July 9, 2002).

4. Helen Manning. The Corporate Librarian: Great Return on Investment, in James M. Matarazzo et al. (Eds.). *President's Task Force on the Value of the Information Professional*. Final Report. Preliminary Study. Washington, DC: Special Libraries Association, 1987, 23–34.

5. Jose-Marie Griffiths and Donald W. King. *Special Libraries: Increasing the Information Edge*. Washington, DC: Special Libraries Association, 1993.

6. Gwen Harris and Joanne G. Marshall. Building a Model Business Case: Current Awareness Service in a Special Library. *Special Libraries*, 87 (2), Summer 1996, 181–94.

7. Marshall, *Impact of the Special Library on Corporate Decision-Making*.

8. Mary Corcoran and Anthea Stratigos. *Knowledge Management: It's All About Behavior. Information About Information Briefing*. Burlingame, CA: Outsell, January 2001.

9. Note that these numbers represent 1993 data and that some adjustment for inflation may need to be made should a library wish to present this information to its funding decision makers.

10. Alison M. Keyes. The Value of the Special Library: Review and Analysis. *Special Libraries*, 86 (3), Summer 1995, 172–87.

11. Leigh Estabrook. Valuing a Document Delivery System. *Research Quarterly*, 27 (1), Fall 1986, 59–62.

12. Manning, The Corporate Librarian.

13. Michael Koenig. The Importance of Information Services for Productivity "Under-Recognized" and Under-Invested. *Special Libraries*, 83 (3), Fall 1992, 199–210.

14. Margareta Nelke. Swedish Corporations Value Information. *Information Outlook*, 3 (2), February 1999, 10.

15. Joanne Gard Marshall. The Impact of the Hospital Library on Clinical Decision-Making: The Rochester Study. *Bulletin of the Medical Library Association*. 80 (2), 1992, 169–78.

16. Marshall, *Impact of the Special Library on Corporate Decision-Making*.

17. Joanne Gard Marshall. Health Canada Libraries, in Elizabeth Orna (Ed.). *Practical Information Policies*. New York: Gower, 1999; and Joanne Gard Marshall. Determining Our Worth, Communicating Our Value. *Library Journal*, 125 (19), November 15, 2000, 29–30.

18. Koenig, The Importance of Information Services for Productivity, 199–210.

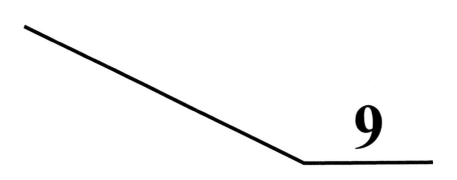

# 9

# A Balanced Scorecard

*If you want to do something new, you have to stop doing something old.*

—Peter Drucker

The mission of any special library is to provide and deliver information for the needs of a specific population. Aside from the use of certain performance measures for internal management use, libraries have tended to report a "mish-mash" of measures to their funding decision makers. Historically, the reported measures have been indirect measures of the value of library services, such as use of the collection, the accuracy of service delivery, the speed of delivering information, the cost efficiency of a library's services and products, and the satisfaction rate of the clients. The often unstated assumption about why these indirect measures are being reported is that high use of the library indicates real benefits to the users of the library, that quick and accurate delivery enhances these benefits, that the library is well-organized and efficient, and that client satisfaction points to good performance.

Starting in the 1990s, companies began to realize that they needed to report more than the traditional financial measures, for example, profits, return-on-capital employed, and so forth, that they had historically used in filings with the Securities and Exchange Commission (SEC) and with their shareholders in the form of an annual report. Intangible assets of an organization began to become more important as the rules governing noncompetitive environments were being changed. Issues about maintaining customer relationships, enhancing service and product quality, motivating and mobilizing employees so that they were more responsive to needs of customers, and environmental concerns were coming to the forefront.

Kaplan and Norton first introduced the idea of a "balanced scorecard" in 1992 in the *Harvard Business Review* and then followed this up with two books on the topic.[1] They developed the "balanced scorecard"concept to add a set of complementary measures to the existing financial measures used by most organizations. The financial measures produced by an accounting system are backward-looking and, by their very nature, report history: what happened last month, last quarter, last year, and so forth. The goal of the balanced scorecard is to identify a set of measures that reflect future performance. Thus, the objectives and measures for the balanced scorecard are chosen from an organization's vision and strategy and include financial, customer, internal business process, and innovation and learning (sometimes called potentials). Within each broad category, three to five measures are chosen to present a clearer picture of that area.

The balanced scorecard approach is not meant to be restrictive. All four categories should only be used if they are appropriate. Further, if the needs of an organization require it, one or more perspectives can be added or subtracted. For example, Deakin University in Australia added a fifth perspective, information resources, when the library developed its balanced scorecard. Other organizations have added a fifth area, competitors, to their scorecards. Neely and Adams have developed a "performance prism" in which they also suggest using five perspectives.[2] Schiemann and Lingle feel that there should be six perspectives: market, financial, people, operations, environment, and partners/suppliers.[3] However, the four perspectives described by Kaplan and Norton are generally applicable in a wide range of organizations and form an excellent starting point for the development of a balanced scorecard in any library.

An alternative approach to a scorecard design is to use the Baldrige Award criteria. However, winning of the Baldrige Award does not necessarily guarantee success as measured by the ultimate yardstick: success earned in the competitive marketplace. Strassmannn has noted that few Baldrige Award winners add real economic value after the company has won the award (and one firm even filed for bankruptcy two years after winning the award).[4] Thus, focusing solely on quality will not necessarily result in better long-term success for any organization. The Kaplan and Norton approach, which includes measures of innovation, learning, and growth, is recommended for use in libraries.

# THE BALANCED SCORECARD: AN EXPLANATION

The balanced scorecard concept can be developed in parallel with the planning process of most organizations. The function of a balanced scorecard is to identify the key metrics across all levels of an organization with the fundamental purpose of aligning organizational goals and objectives with the activities at the operating levels. The organization can select scorecard performance measures that have a broad perspective that can, in turn, be linked to the planning process.

The balanced scorecard concept has been successfully applied in a number of settings, including libraries (see Figures 9.1 and 9.2, page 106). The balanced scorecard does not assist a library in developing a strategy, goals, and objectives nor is it a process improvement methodology. Rather, it is a series of indicators (think of your elementary school report card) to tell you how you are doing. However, in order to be truly beneficial, there should be a link between the library's balanced scorecard and the strategies being used to deliver quality services. The scorecard encourages a library to translate its vision into terms that have meaning to the staff members who would realize the vision.

The basic features of a measurement-based management system, such as the balanced scorecard, are

Specification of one or more objectives for each "perspective,"

Definition of a quantitative metric or "score,"

A target value,

A target date, and

A periodic measurement cycle.

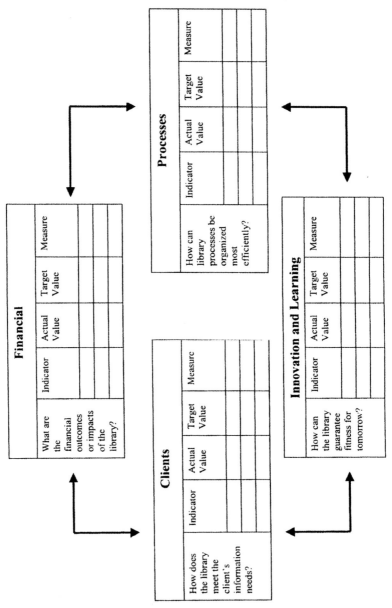

Figure 9.1. The Library Balanced Scorecard. Adapted from "Performance, Processes and Costs: Managing Service Quality with the Balanced Scorecard" by Roswitha Poll, *Library Trends* Volume 49, Number 4, pp. 709–717. Copyright © 2001 The Board of Trustees of the University of Illinois. Reprinted with Permission. See also the University of Virginia library's Balanced Scorecard, available at:
http://staff.lib.Virginia.edu/management-information/bsc.html.

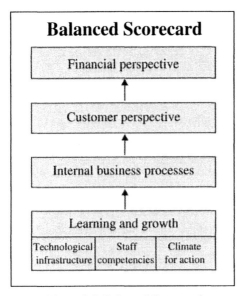

**Figure 9.2. Balanced Scorecard**

These measures must be selected so that they are indicators that can be influenced directly by managers and staff of the library, thus encouraging changes in behavior that will assist in achieving organizational goals. In addition, each potential measure should be assessed to determine whether it currently is being collected or if it will require a new, and potentially costly, data-gathering process.

# Financial Perspective

For-profit organizations typically have financial themes that govern business strategy, which might include

Revenue growth and mix,

Profitability,

Shareholder value,

Cost reduction or productivity improvement, and

Asset utilization or an investment strategy.

The special library, whether a part of a for-profit company, a nonprofit organization, or a governmental agency, can demonstrate its financial value by asking its customers to identify the impact of using a library service. Financial performance measures indicate whether a library's strategy, implementation, and execution are contributing to the bottom line of the organization. A library implementing a balanced scorecard may want to consider labeling this perspective "business value" or "organizational value" rather than "financial."

The importance of the measures included in the *financial perspective* is that they move beyond demonstrating that the library is managing its resources (inputs) in a cost-efficient manner. For special libraries, it is important to show what the library's outcomes or impacts are from the financial perspective on the larger organization. Usually these outcomes can be categorized by their impact of saving time for the customer, reducing costs, or generating new revenues. For the special library in a for-profit firm, all objectives and measures in the other perspectives should be linked to achieving one or more objectives in the financial or business value perspective.

Some of the candidate measures for the financial perspective to consider are

- Total cost of the library per professional employee,
- Library budget as a percent of the organization's total budget,
- Total amount of savings due to information provided by the library and resulting cost-benefit ratio,
- Total amount of customer time saved due to library services,
- Total increase in revenues for the organization due to library services,
- Total cost of library service per document used (circulation, in-library use, documents examined online),
- Total cost of the library per library visit,
- Cost of materials acquired (acquisitions plus ILL plus document delivery plus subscriptions to online databases) compared to total,
- Percent of acquisitions expenditures spent on electronic media,
- Library staff costs compared to total library budget, and
- Expenditures for circulating monographs as a percent of all monographs (indicates the degree to which current acquisitions are meeting customer needs).

## Client or Customer Perspective

For any organization, the center of any business strategy is the customer value proposition that allows the organization to differentiate itself from its competitors. In general, there are three possible differentiators:

- **Customer intimacy.** Knowledge of the information needs of the different groups of a library's customers allows the library to become more responsive. Note that it is possible for a library or information center to move toward customer intimacy using personalization of services as a strategy. The personalization capabilities would, at a minimum, mimic the services found on Amazon.com: "more like this" recommendations, reviews (published and submitted by colleagues within the organization), alert services, and so forth.

- **Product/service (innovation) leadership.** A library provides access to a number of information products, either in print or online. Examples of library products are the library catalog, pathfinders, subject guides, and bibliographies. However, the customers of the library primarily use library services. For example, customers are interested in gaining access to the information resources found in the library's collection and access to full-text databases.

- **Operational excellence.** The product/service attributes that result from operational excellence include price, quality, selection, and timeliness. Historically the primary benefit of a library is that it assembles a collection of quality information resources, which reduces the time needed for an individual within an organization to find the desired information.

Customer-related measures that have utility across a broad range of organizations include

Market share,

Customer retention,

The acquisition of new customers,

Customer satisfaction, and

Customer profitability.

The indicators chosen for the *client perspective* are measures that show the extent to which the library is serving its potential audience (market share) and how well the client's information needs are being met by the services provided by the library. It is important that these measures reflect the value proposition: how the library creates value for its customers. Generally customer concerns fall into three discrete categories: time, performance and service quality, and cost— all measured from the customer's perspective:

- **Time**. Time has an impact on the customer in several ways. The customer may need to physically visit the library, which will take transportation time. The customer may need to wait in a queue for an opportunity to express an information need. It may take time to fulfill the information need (item on loan, item needs to be ordered via document delivery, and so forth). From the customer's perspective the time and energy necessary to fulfill an information need should not become an impediment to seeking library services. The library should ask its customers what timeframe will best meet their needs and then routinely meet and exceed those expectations. Ultimately, the customer makes a decision about whether the effort involved exceeds the likely value of the information being sought.

- **Performance and service.** Performance and service are related concepts that focus on what the service does for the customer and how well it does it. Often measures for performance and service include a client satisfaction survey, although objective measures should also be employed. The provision of ongoing quality services is primarily dependent on continuously improving processes.

- **Cost or price.** Although it is important to provide cost-effective, quality library services, the customer also incurs a cost when seeking to fulfill an information need. Customers evaluate library services when they make decisions about how to spend their time and attention. Thus, the library will be considered as but one option unless the value of the library services is so great that competitors are not seriously considered.[5]

The client perspective should capture the views of clients who directly receive the services as well as stakeholders who judge the success and utility of the library. The client perspective allows a library to determine what segments of its possible customer base it is actually serving. Client perspective measures include

- Market penetration—percent of clients compared to total possible population to be served;
- Percent of clients that have used the library in the last six months, by client type;
- Total hours the library is open per week
- Amount of use of the library's collection (circulation, in-library use, documents examined online);
- Collection availability rate;
- Collection turnover rate;
- Percent of professionals using electronic library services;
- Measures of use of specific electronic resources;
- Amount of use of reference services;
- Reference transactions per 1,000 of possible population;
- Amount of use of document delivery;
- Circulation of new monographs compared to all monographs;
- Time to fulfill user requests; and
- A user satisfaction survey.

# Internal Process Perspective

Measures reflecting the *internal processes perspective* should be selected to demonstrate that the library is managing its resources in an efficient way. More important, the process measures selected should be those that will have the greatest impact on the clients. Quality improvement initiatives attempt to monitor and improve existing library processes. The scorecard approach may, however, identify new processes at which the library must excel to meet customer expectations and changing conditions in the marketplace. For example, conducting a series of focus groups with nonlibrary customers may identify some innovative services that would convert these individuals to library customers.

The goal here is to understand the processes that are critical to enabling the library to satisfy its customers' needs and the processes that add value in the customers' eyes. It is not unusual for cost, quality, throughput, productivity, and time measures to be defined and measured for this perspective. Among the measures that might be included in this section are

- Percent of reference questions answered correctly;
- TSCORE (total salaries for technical services divided by the collection materials budget);
- Cost to acquire, catalog, and process an item for the library's collection (compared to "similar" libraries or as a percent of the library's budget);
- Time to acquire, catalog, and process an item for the library's collection;
- Time to purchase a document using document delivery;
- Turnaround time to shelve books; and
- Percent of staff time spent on electronic services.

A library's exclusive focus on improving internal processes, such as benchmarking efforts that focus on the productivity of staff members, may be misplaced. Since most organizations are focused, in part, on improving quality and productivity, a library will likely find that it is merely maintaining the status quo with its competitors. Rather, the library should be identifying and implementing strategies that allow it to offer distinctive and sustainable competitive advantages.

The focus may be on continuous improvement of existing processes, or the library may decide that it needs a radical process redesign such as that advocated by Hammer and Champy.[6] The focal point of process reengineering is not efficiency (although efficiency will most likely be improved), but rather effectiveness: what is going to add value for the customers. Some of the tools used by organizations to assist in a process reengineering project are activity modeling, data modeling, ABC, and cost-benefit analysis.

# Innovation and Learning Perspective

The perspective labeled *"innovation and learning"* or *"potentials"* focuses on the ability of the library to change and improve and answers the question: "How can the library continue to improve and add value?" This perspective also identifies the infrastructure that the library needs to sustain and improve its service offerings. The innovation dimension helps libraries remain forward focused by evaluating their ability to improve, innovate, and learn.

Measures might include the levels of institutional support, communications and information technology support (if this is a library responsibility), staff development and training, employee motivation, retention, and empowerment. This perspective can be grouped into three categories, as shown in Figure 9.2.

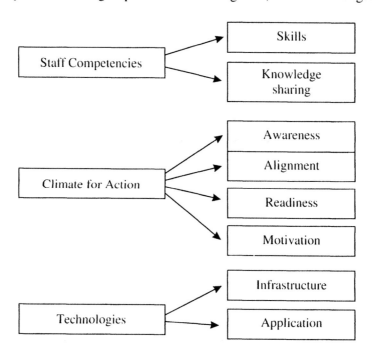

**Figure 9.3. Innovation and Learning Perspective**

This perspective attempts to answer the following questions:

- Are staff members qualified and equipped with the right skills to deliver quality results?

- Are new skills being tracked that are important to the library and organization's mission?

- Is a consistent and effective methodology being used to track the results of projects?

- Do staff have the proper tools, training, and incentives to perform their tasks?

- Do staff understand the use of the measures in the balanced scorecard and how the measures relate to the library's strategies?

The development of measures for this perspective may reveal gaps between the existing capabilities of people, procedures, and technology and what may be required. Generally it is important for staff members to improve their technology skills on an ongoing basis since technology applications are always changing. It may be necessary to invest in staff training, enhancing information technology and systems, and realigning of the library's procedures and processes. The expectation is that focusing on innovation and learning will ultimately have a positive impact on performance, as shown in Figure 9.3.

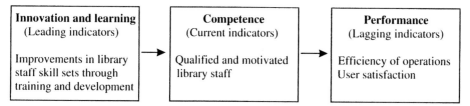

**Figure 9.4. Innovation and Learning Leads to Future Performance Improvements**

Given the wide range of possible measures, a library might want to consider

- The information and communications technology budget as a percent of the institution's budget (or library's budget),
- Network and system reliability measures,
- Reliability of equipment,
- The number of formal training hours per staff member,
- The number of formal training hours provided by library staff,
- A staff satisfaction survey,
- The retention rate among "key" employees,
- The Human Capital Index (a composite measure that consists of number of years worked in a library, level within the organization performance rating, and number and variety of positions/assignments held), and
- The number of short-term illnesses per staff member.

The selection of which and how many measures to include in the library balanced scorecard is a balancing act. On the one hand, too many measures will begin to confuse the library's funding decision makers (Which measures should the managers pay attention to?); on the other hand, too few measures will not provide a robust and representative view of the library and its information services. The intent of the balanced scorecard concept is to integrate a set of complementary measures to go beyond the traditional input, process, and output-oriented measures and reflect the real impacts or outcomes of the library on the larger organization or community.

All of these measures provide valuable information about the health of a library. Given that no single measure or perspective is enough by itself, the use of four perspectives provides the "balance" in the balanced scorecard.

# INTELLECTUAL CAPITAL VALUATION

Portugal suggested a similar approach to the library balanced scorecard in *Valuing Information Intangibles.*[7] He called this approach "intellectual capital valuation" and suggested using a total of 15 measures grouped into five categories (user or client focus, process focus, renewal and development focus, human focus, and financial focus), as shown in Table 9.1.

## Table 9.1. Intellectual Capital Valuation

| Metric | 1998 | 1999 | 2000 |
|---|---|---|---|
| **User or Client (Customer) Focus** | | | |
| Number of library users | 1,112 | 1,237 | 1,379 |
| Annual Revenue/Library User ($) | 1,700 | 1,722 | 1,754 |
| Average Library User Rating of Library (1–10) | 7.1 | 7.3 | 8.5 |
| | | | |
| **Process Focus** | | | |
| Administrative Expense/Total Revenue (%) | 20.1 | 23.4 | 24.5 |
| Average Processing Time for Searches (minutes) | 47 | 59 | 65 |
| Information Technology Capacity of Library (GB) | 20.3 | 30.6 | 40.4 |
| | | | |
| **Renewal and Development Focus** | | | |
| Employee Satisfaction Rating (1–5) | 3.7 | 3.1 | 2.9 |
| Noncompetency Training Expense/Library Employee ($) | 435 | 527 | 540 |
| User Base Captured/Total Opportunity User Base (%) | 24 | 25 | 26 |

| Metric | 1998 | 1999 | 2000 |
|---|---|---|---|
| **Human Focus** | | | |
| Empowered Library Staff (%) | 52 | 49 | 44 |
| Average Age of Library Employees (years) | 43 | 44 | 46 |
| Annual Turnover of Full-time Permanent Employees (%) | 7 | 13 | 4 |
| | | | |
| **Financial Focus** | | | |
| Library Profits/Total Library Assets (%) | 14.2 | 15.5 | 4.2 |
| Library Revenue New Business ($) | 105,499 | 107,364 | 108,000 |
| Profits Added/Library Employee ($) | 110,000 | 112,349 | 114,588 |

*Source:* **Adapted from Frank Portugal.** *Valuing Information Intangibles: Measuring the Bottom Line Contribution of Librarians and Information Professionals.* **Washington, DC: Special Libraries Association, 2000, 75.**

The value of the library balanced scorecard approach is that it assists librarians in identifying what measures are important and supports the presentation of these measures in a cogent and understandable form for the management team of the larger organization. Furthermore, the data collection process and use of these measures does not require the use of a consultant or researcher. Rather, once the process is established, the data for each of the measures can be assembled in a straightforward manner and without a great deal of effort. Once collected, the measures can be presented in a written report to provide to the library's funding decision makers and other interested parties.

# PRESENTATION OF THE LIBRARY'S BALANCED SCORECARD

Rather than relying on a presentation of the balanced scorecard as shown in Figure 9.1 (page 106), the information can be viewed in graphical form, as shown in Figure 9.5. This graphical view of the balanced scorecard is sometimes called a "dashboard" because the indicators resemble the instruments found on a dashboard in an automobile. The "arrow" indicates the current assessment for a particular perspective, and the "bar" indicates the target or goal.

When a dashboard presentation is planned, the challenge is to convert dissimilar measures (each measure may be using a different metric, for example, dollars, cost per transaction, Likert scale, and count) into an arbitrary scale, such as low-to-high or 0-to-10, as one would find on an automobile gauge.

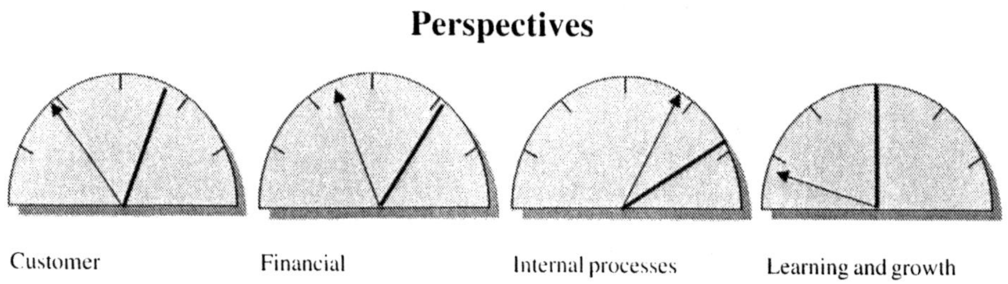

## Perspectives

| Customer | Financial | Internal processes | Learning and growth |

**Figure 9.5. "Dashboard" View of a Balanced Scorecard**

Each measure must be "fitted" or scaled so that one measure's metric can be converted into the arbitrary scale to be used by the dashboard instrument, for example 1 to 10, 1 to 5, -2 to +2, and so forth. As shown in Table 9.2 (page 117), some creativity is needed to ensure that the range for each measure (low value, current value, target value, and high value) is included in the "converted" scale.

Next, the library should determine whether each of four measures used for a particular perspective should be equally weighted or one or more measures assigned a disproportionate weighting. Table 9.2 assumes that a disproportionate weighting is used. (Note that the total weights must equal 100 in this case. The total might be 10 if that was the range of the scale for the "instrument.")

# CONCERNS

Several concerns have been raised about the balanced scorecard approach,[8] including the following:

- **Sponsorship**. Where does the impetus for using a balanced scorecard originate? Is there active participation among library staff and library funding decision makers (stakeholders) about the need for and value of such an approach? Is the balanced scorecard being introduced in the larger organizational setting?

- **Strategies and objectives**. Are the strategies, goals, and objectives for the library in place? Are they clearly defined, well known, and understood among library staff and among library funding decision makers?

- **Decision-making style**. Are decisions made in a formal or unstructured setting? Are decisions made centrally, or are they decentralized?

- **Information availability**. Is the information collected in a consistent manner so that there is confidence in the metrics? Is the information used to populate the measures in place? Are the measures objective? Is the library currently collecting a plethora of measures? Are only some of these measures actually being used?

- **Competing initiatives**. Are there any other projects that will distract the library or the library's funding decision makers from focusing on the balanced scorecard project?

**Table 9.2. Sample Scaling to Create a Dashboard Instrument**

| Measure | Type of Metric | Range of Metric | Value of Current Metric | "Converted" Value | Weighted (percent) | Weighted Value |
|---|---|---|---|---|---|---|
| Percent of clients compared to total number of possible clients | Proportion | 0–100% | 60 | 6.0 | 20 | 1.2 |
| Total amount of use | Count | 0–150,000 | 90,000 | 6.0 | 20 | 1.2 |
| Number of reference transactions per 1,000 possible clients | Ratio | 0–10.0 | 7.0 | 7.0 | 40 | 2.8 |
| User satisfaction survey | Likert | 1–7 | 6.1 | 8.7 | 40 | 3.5 |
| | | | | | | |
| Total | | | | | | 8.7 |

*Note:* **Maximum possible score = 12**

- **Lack of a common denominator**. Since nonfinancial data are measured in many ways—time, counts, percent, and so forth—there is no consistent basis for the use of all measures. Some organizations have attempted to overcome this problem through the use of weighted averages and arbitrary weightings, but these approaches are subjective and can lead to problems.

# SUMMARY

The use of a balanced scorecard offers the opportunity to use a "family" of measures that are designed to target how well the organization or library is doing from four perspectives. This approach means that the library need not try to identify the best one or two measures but rather can select a set of measures that are designed to complement one another. The use of the balanced scorecard provides an integrated view of financial and nonfinancial measures, leading and laggard indicators, as well as an external perspective (funding and customers) and an internal perspective (process and potentials). The end result is a set of measures that should show how the library is providing real value to its parent organization. There are many aspects to providing library services, and the balanced scorecard provides an integrated view of library and information services.

# NOTES

1. Robert S. Kaplan and David P. Norton. The Balanced Scorecard—Measures That Drive Performance. *Harvard Business Review*, 70 (1), 1992, 71–79; Robert S. Kaplan and David P. Norton. *The Balanced Scorecard*. Boston: Harvard Business School Press, 1996; and Robert S. Kaplan and David P. Norton. *The Strategy-Focused Organization: How Balanced Scorecard Companies Thrive in the New Business Environment*. Boston: Harvard Business School Press, 2001.

2. Andy Neely and Chris Adams. Perspectives on Performance: The Performance Prism. *Focus Magazine*, 4, August 2000. Available at http://www.focusmag.com/pages/senexec.htm (accessed July 9, 2002).

3. William A. Schiemann and John H. Lingle. *Bullseye!* Hitting Your Strategic Targets Through High-Impact Measurements. New York: Free Press, 1999.

4. Paul A. Strassmann. *The Squandered Computer: Evaluating the Business Alignment of Information Technologies*. New Canaan, CT: The Information Economics Press, 1997.

5. Charles Birch. *Future Success: A Balanced Approach to Measuring and Improving Success in Your Organization*. New York: Prentice Hall Press, 2000.

6. Michael Hammer and James Champy. *Reengineering the Corporation: A Manifesto for Business Revolution*. New York: HarperBusiness, 1993. See also David Osborne and Ted Gaebler. *Reinventing Government: How the Entrepreneurial Spirit Is Transforming the Public Sector*. New York: Addison-Wesley, 1992.

7. Frank Portugal. *Valuing Information Intangibles: Measuring the Bottom Line Contribution of Librarians and Information Professionals*. Washington, DC: Special Libraries Association, 2000, 75.

8. Earl Hadden. Orchestrate a Concerted Effort. *Intelligent Enterprise*, 2, July 13, 1999, 22–25.

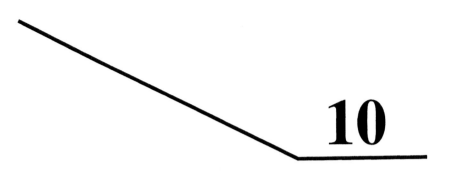

# Building a Library
# Balanced Scorecard

*To be successful the Balanced Scorecard must be viewed as the tip of the improvement iceberg.*

—A. M. Schnneiderman

A balanced scorecard is more than selecting three to four performance measures for each perspective. The reality of this approach is all that would be accomplished is the adoption of multiple measures, some of which might actually be in conflict with one another. The special library should follow a process that links the selection of specific performance measures to the strategic goals and objectives of the library, as shown in Figure 10.1 (page 120).

This top-down approach allows the library to link measures to strategies and, more specifically, works to ensure that the performance measures actually have a cause-and-effect relationship, that is, each of the measures is linked one to another as well as to the strategies being used by the library to achieve its vision.

The library balanced scorecard will assist the library in communicating its value to interested stakeholders, and it can be used to support the planning process by providing feedback on how well the library is doing in meeting its objectives. The use of multidimensional metrics will change the perspective when assessing the library's performance—*away from* past performance *toward* what the library seeks to become.

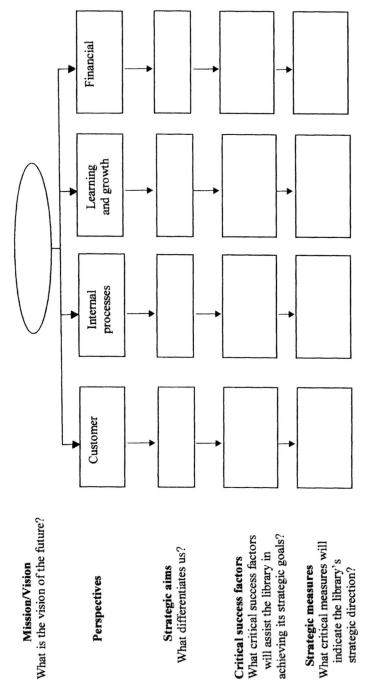

Figure 10.1. Overview of the Process to Create a Library Balanced Scorecard

# MISSION STATEMENT

Prior to starting the process to develop a library balanced scorecard, the library may wish to review and update its mission statement, which reflects the goals of its organization. The library should engage in a process of planning before it even begins to consider the prospect of identifying and using a set of performance measures. Ensuring that the library or information center is aligned with the goals and objectives of its parent organization is almost self-evident and yet, even today, a mismatch persists in some libraries.

Jones suggests that the process of business planning—in some organizations it might be called strategic planning, establishing priorities, program planning, or direction planning—clarifies why the library exists, who it exists for, what services and products are provided to different groups of clients, how these products and services will be evaluated, and where it is going.[1] Figure 10.2 provides a generalized view of the planning process and illustrates the interdependent relationships among each of the components:

- **Rationale**. Why does the parent organization exist? Why does the library continue to provide services? What is the organization's mission statement?

- **Vision**. Where is the organization headed? What is the appropriate role for the library to play?

- **Market**. What groups does the library serve? Do remote users have access to the same set of resources as those who physically visit the library?

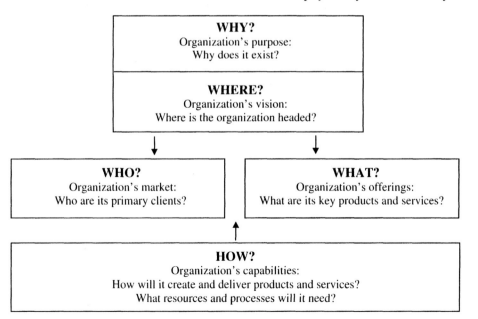

**Figure 10.2. Planning Framework**

- **Offerings**. What products and services does the library provide?
- **Capabilities**. What resources are required to provide the services and products the library offers: technology, space, people, and processes?

The clarity of an organization's mission statement is crucial so that all staff members have a clear understanding of the goals and direction of the organization. Too often a committee will craft an organization's mission statement and the results will be usually something less than helpful. When evaluating a mission statement, note that it should

- Define what the organization does and does not do,
- Distinguish your organization from the competition,
- Be no more than a short paragraph in length (one sentence is better),
- Be written in plain English and employ no buzzwords,
- Lead to clear actions, and
- Focus on the present—it's not a future-focused vision statement.

The purpose of the mission statement is to clearly articulate the special library's role in the company or organization. One broad generic statement of purpose or mission for the special library might be that the library offers an information infrastructure of resources and services that supports the role of the organization. The library should actively involve a number of library customers in developing or revising its mission statement to ensure that the needs of its customers are well known and addressed in the planning process.

# VISION STATEMENT

Part of the planning process is to create a formal statement of vision, which describes how the library is expected to be three to five years later. The vision sets out long-term targets and success criteria for the library and acts as a focus for identifying the key strategic activities that need to be accomplished if the vision is to be achieved.[2]

An important first step in any planning process is to assess the environment within which the organization exists. Assessing the context of the current and likely future environment helps to determine what factors will affect the parent organization and, in turn, the library. What industry trends, government regulations, and technology changes will affect the organization? Who are the library's competitors, and how well is the organization doing in the competitive environment? One of the most popular planning tools to assist in this process is called SWOT: identifying the strengths, weaknesses, opportunities, and threats of/to the library.

Once an assessment has been made of the external factors that will likely have an impact on the organization, attention shifts to an internal focus. After the factors for each of these areas have been identified and assessed, the library can complete the preparation of its plan.

A part of the vision statement should address any concerns about actual or potential competition that the library is currently facing or likely to encounter in the next few years. For example, the library might conclude that the popularity of the Internet and the organization's intranet should be recognized, even indirectly, and thus its new mission statement might be: "Provide convenient in-person and online access to a variety of materials and information resources to all employees."

In short, the library, as a part of its planning process, should be able to answer six key questions:

- *What* do we do?
- *Who* do we do it for?
- What do they *want* and why?
- How can we better *improve* their satisfaction and the library's performance?
- What is the *strategy* and *process* for delivering library services?
- Do we know or can we determine the library's contribution to the success of the organization?

## STRATEGIC AIMS

Some organizations have attempted to find the "right or correct" strategy in the hope that that is what is needed to succeed. Interestingly, an examination of why some companies, and their CEOs, failed leads to the conclusion that the real problem isn't bad strategy but rather bad execution.[3] Michael Porter, a well-known expert in the area of strategic planning, has noted that strategy cannot be limited to those at the top of an organization but rather must involve all staff members as they go about completing their tasks.[4]

In the past, the goals and objectives of a library have not been linked to the performance measures gathered by the library, as evidenced by a library's annual plan of programs and initiatives—with no links to performance measures. The implications of this fact are significant. The reality is that there is a total disconnect between the daily actions of managers and the activities of staff members and the library's mission statement and vision for the future. The majority of performance measurements systems are designed around the annual budget and operating plan. This results in short-term, incremental behavior.

*Think of strategy as a bridge: values are the bedrock on which the piers of the bridge are planted, the near bank is today's reality, the far bank is the vision. Your strategy is the bridge itself.*

**—Gordon R. Sullivan**[5]

Performance measures are designed to assist the library in determining if it is moving in the right direction. Strategy is not about destination but about the route the library chooses to take: *how* to reach the desired destination.

If a library wishes to consider adopting a set of strategies that will be most responsive to its customers, there are three broad avenues to consider: customer intimacy, innovative services, and operational excellence. These broad avenues are interrelated, as shown in Figure 10.3. Having a greater understanding of the needs of the library's customers and how the library adds value will allow the library to develop new innovative services. As these services are incorporated into the routine library service offerings, they will be more highly appreciated and valued by the customers of the library.

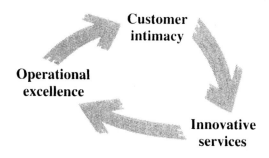

**Figure 10.3. Interrelationships of Service Strategies**

To create superior value, two types of knowledge are required: having a clear understanding of what customers value and knowing what skills are necessary to respond to customer needs. One of the obvious ways to discover more about the needs of the library's actual and potential customers is to segment this group into three or more groups: frequent users, infrequent users, and nonusers. Gathering a representative sample for a group, the library could conduct a focus group interview to discover the ways in which the library could add value to its service offerings so that the individual is more likely to benefit from using one or more library services. A separate focus group meeting should be held for each segment. A larger group of individuals could be involved in a PAPE survey to complement the results of the focus group meetings.

After the library has a better understanding of the needs of the people in the larger organization, the library could explore developing and evaluating new and innovative services. A range of services could potentially be introduced that would appeal to different segments of customers. Some of these strategic approaches are shown in Table 10.1 using the added-value attributes identified by Taylor that a library uses when it provides a service and the three broad avenues of strategy formulation suggested previously. These potential strategies are meant to be illustrative, not exhaustive.

## Table 10.1. Potential Strategies

| | Customer Intimacy | Service Innovation | Operational Excellence |
|---|---|---|---|
| Ease of use | Increase range of information resources | Simplified searching (automatically search multiple databases)<br><br>Provide online services that are equivalent to in-library services | Reduce barriers to access<br><br>—the collection<br>—online databases<br>—reference services |
| Noise reduction | Improve use of filters<br><br>Develop Pathfinders | Improve alert services<br><br>Adding extensive cross-references<br><br>Adding enhanced MARC records<br><br>Adding quality MARC records for Internet-based resources | Exceed expectations |
| Quality | Improve customer profile | Develop a presearch database<br><br>Adding a "more like this" search capability | Improve accuracy of reference services<br><br>Improve consistency of service offerings<br><br>Improve the quality of the library's bibliographic and authority records |
| Adaptability | Increase range of services<br><br>Customer segmentation | Librarian becomes an active member of all teams<br><br>Develop a summarization service | Provide flexible service options |
| Time savings | Provide "express lane" service offerings | Improve personalization options<br><br>Improve customer economics | Reduce processing speeds<br><br>Improve library staff productivity<br><br>Deliver as-promised |
| Cost savings | Understanding the "cost drivers" of the organization | Bundle solutions<br><br>Track cost savings ideas in "our" industry | Work with suppliers to reduce costs<br><br>Identify ways to use the collection more (improved asset utilization) |

The objective in this part of the process of developing a library balanced scorecard is to convert the mission of the library into more specific strategic aims for each perspective. The library may wish to identify two or three more narrowly defined strategies that pertain to all customers or it may want to have different strategies for several different types of customers. Each library will want to carefully examine a range of possible strategies that it might use to meet the needs of its customers.

It should be noted that strategies are *not* the programmatic goals and objectives that most libraries have historically developed on an annual basis. A strategy is a plan of action with a shared understanding designed to accomplish a specific goal. For example, some libraries develop programmatic goals that are grouped into several categories (services, technology, resources, staff development). Such an approach does not reflect a coherent set of strategies but is rather a potpourri of goals and objectives. Goals and objectives for each perspective that emerge from a strategic planning process will be linked to a particular strategy. In short, there is a cause and effect relationship between strategy and the measures ultimately selected for each perspective.

After the library has developed a set of strategies that it would like to pursue for the next few years, the library director will want to review these strategies with his or her funding decision makers and other important stakeholders so that there is understanding and consensus about the approach being taken by the library to develop its library balanced scorecard.

# CRITICAL SUCCESS FACTORS

The next step in the process, as shown in Figure 10.1 (page 120), is to identify the critical success factors (sometimes called key success factors). A critical success factor is one of the characteristics that is essential to the success of the library and distinguishes the library from its competitors.[6] Some of the potential critical success factors for a library are

| | |
|---|---|
| Responsive service | Quality service |
| Availability of information resources | Search intermediary skills |
| Consistency of service | Improving the productivity of customers |
| Leading-edge technology | Customization service |
| Service for remote customers equivalent to being on-site | Alerting service |

When trying to identify its critical success factors, the library should be able to answer each of the following questions:

• Why do customers use the library (both physically and electronically)?

- Why do some customers return repeatedly and some don't come back?
- Why do some individuals never use the library, either physically or electronically?
- What advantages does the library have over its competitors?
- What weaknesses come to mind when the library and its services are being evaluated or considered?
- What words come to mind when people think about the library?
- What does the special library want to be known for?
- What new services should the library introduce?
- How can the library add more value to its existing or planned services?
- Are there one or more existing services that can be safely eliminated?

The library may wish to create a team to generate a list of critical success factors via a brainstorming session, then prioritize these factors. The most effective way to rate each of these critical success factors is to indicate the degree to which it will influence the strategies that have been selected. It is important that a critical success factor be measured using objective criteria. Among the characteristics of good critical success factors are the following:

- They are directly linked to the mission.
- These factors are not financial goals, targets, or measures.
- They are what differentiates the library from its competitors.
- They are clearly defined and easily understood.

Differentiation arises from both the choice of service activities and how they are performed. Critical success factors have been combined with the value chain concept to form an information audit that identifies the information needs of an organization.[7]

# STRATEGIC MEASURES

Use of the balanced scorecard approach allows the special library to clearly indicate what is important through its choice of the measures included in the scorecard. Making sure that the "appropriate" set of measures reflects the goals and objectives of the library is what the planning process is all about. Using the balanced scorecard on a quarterly basis allows all staff members to see how the library is doing toward achieving its goals (and to take corrective action, if needed).[8] The measures in the library balanced scorecard should have a cause-and-effect relationship that communicates the meaning of the strategy to library staff members and to the larger organization, as shown in Figure 10.4 (page 128).

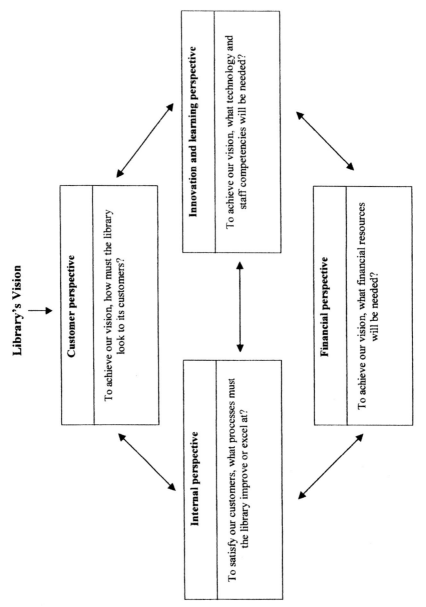

**Figure 10.4. Cause-and-Effect Relationship of Strategy**

For special libraries that are a part of a for-profit organization, the process of establishing the cause-and-effect relationships should, in most cases, start with the *financial perspective*. The goal here is to demonstrate that the library is efficiently using the financial resources provided to the library as well as to identify the positive outcomes that result from the library's information services (value of time saved, cost savings, and an increase of revenues).

Special libraries that are part of a not-for-profit organization may decide that the most important focus is the *customer perspective*. What segments of the employees in the larger organization is the library currently serving? What groups does the library want to target? How does each group of customers define a quality library? How does the library differentiate itself to attract and retain customers (the value proposition)?

Continuing the top-down process, the *internal processes* define the processes needed to create the desired customer value proposition. The *innovation and learning perspective* acknowledges that the ability to execute internal processes requires an infrastructure that is composed of the skills and knowledge of employees, the technology that they use, and the work environment or climate in which they work.

Critical success factors can be used to assist in the evaluation process of choosing cause-and-effect relationships since it is not unusual to identify a plethora of links.[9] The strategy cause-and-effect links between perspectives must be clear and offer a compelling reason for a choice when compared to other alternatives. In short:

- The strategic goals in the customer perspective should support the achievement of the financial goals.
- The choice of the strategic goals in the process perspective should be linked to realizing the customer goals.
- The goals in the innovation and learning perspective should promote the attainment of the process perspective.

As noted in Chapter 9, at least one library has added another perspective, *information resources*, so that the resources contained in the library's collection as well as the information obtained from external sources, such as online databases, e-journals, and document delivery are also assessed in a systematic manner.

The value of the library balanced scorecard approach is that it assists librarians in identifying what measures are important and supports the presentation of these measures in a cogent and understandable form for the special library's funding decision makers. Furthermore, the data collection process and use of these measures does not require the use of a consultant or researcher. Once the initial library balanced scorecard has been created, the data for each of the measures can be assembled in a straightforward manner. If the collection of data to support a specific performance measure is difficult or time consuming, then use of another measure should be considered. In addition, as the library gains experience in using the scorecard, it will likely fine-tune the scorecard by substituting one measure for another. However, it is important to note that the real value of the balanced scorecard occurs when there is consistency in what measures are used year-to-year and how data for these measures are gathered. Even a slight change can have an adverse impact on the utility of a measure.

Kaplan and Norton suggest that one of the most effective ways to stay focused on strategies is to select performance measures that are linked in a cause-and-effect relationship with measures from other perspectives that are linked to one or more strategies. One useful tool is to create a balanced scorecard strategy map, as shown in Figure 10.5 (page 130).

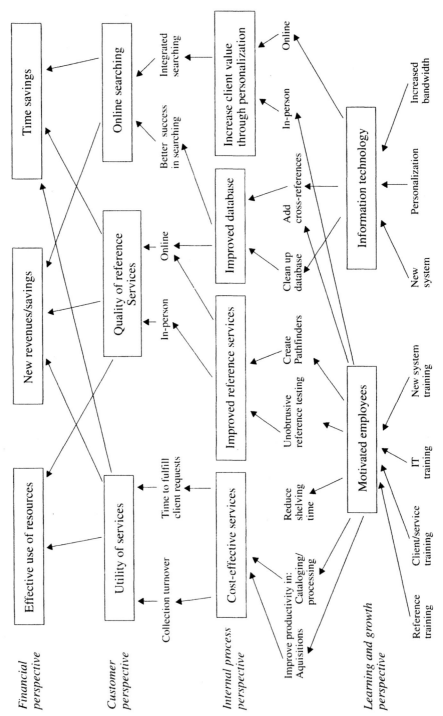

**Figure 10.5. Library Balanced Scorecard Strategy Map**

The strategy map presented here is for a special library that is part of a for-profit organization. A PAPE conducted the previous year indicated that the areas needing improvement were the availability of materials (whether in the collection or obtained via a document delivery service) and improving reference services (both in-person and online). Therefore, the library has established two primary strategies to meet the needs of its customers: (1) reduce the time it takes to acquire, process, and shelve new materials; and (2) solicit more frequent feedback on the adequacy and utility of reference services.

Measures for the financial perspective will demonstrate the financial impact or outcome of the library on the larger organization by identifying new revenues, reduced costs, and improved productivity through time savings that resulted from the use of the library. Library customers will be regularly surveyed to collect this information, and the library will prepare an annual cost-benefit analysis. In addition, the library will use a measure(s) to demonstrate the efficient use of resources.

The measures for the customer perspective are designed to show how responsive the library is to the needs of its customers by asking the customer to participate in a periodic materials availability survey. In addition, customers will be asked to participate in a periodic customer satisfaction survey (remember that library customers had previously participated in a needs assessment or PAPE survey). Reference services, either in-person or online, will be assessed using unobtrusive testing.

The process perspective is focused on measures that reflect the operational efficiency of the library (time and cost to acquire, catalog, and process new materials as well as the quality of reference services) and an initiative to provide more individualized services (whether in-person or online). Improved personalization services will, it is hoped, lead more people within the organization to use library services.

The innovation and learning perspective has a set of measures that focus on encouraging staff growth through a staff needs assessment survey, training, and a staff satisfaction survey. The other measure is designed to determine the level of investment in information technology (which will increasingly be used to provide personalized information services).

The importance of the strategy map is that it helps the library determine if the measures it has selected are actually linked in a cause-and-effect relationship from one perspective to the next. After all, it is the knowledge, skills, and knowledge of processes that library staff members will need (their learning and growth) to innovate. These skills allow staff to build the right capabilities and efficiencies (internal processes) to deliver specific value to the library's customers, which will translate into specific outcomes, which will benefit the organization financially.

The strategy map should ideally be built from the top down so that the appropriate measures are selected to show the links or relationships between the perspectives.

The management team of any organization, including libraries, typically spends very little time each month thinking about and discussing strategies.[10] However, organizations that use the balanced scorecard approach report that their management meetings change from a budget focus to strategy focus. Organizations that use the balanced scorecard find that the ideas and learning that occur during their management meetings help to foster feedback about the progress being made to achieve organizational goals and objectives. In addition, the organization also has the opportunity to fine-tune its strategies in a continual process as circumstances change.

Once the library has embarked on a new course of action that links measurement to strategies, the next step is to make sure that each department within the library also has a plan of action that is consistent with the library's overall goals and objectives. The library management team should ask the following questions:

- Do the measures foster an environment of continuous improvement?

- Are the department's performance measures linked to the strategic objectives of the library?

- Is the performance of the entire library more important than individual department indicators?

- Are the measures from one perspective linked to another perspective?

- Are the library's customers involved in assessing the performance of the library?

- Is time an important measure?

- Does the selection of measures focus on the right priorities? Is there a balance between leading and lagging indicators?

- Do the measures reflect improvements in how work is accomplished?

- Is it possible to capture data for each measure easily and inexpensively?

- Is the balanced scorecard presented in a format that is simple and consistent?

- Is performance compared over time?

- Can the measures be assembled in a timely manner? If the reporting period is quarterly, then the measures should be available for use no longer than one to two weeks after the end of the reporting period.

- Are data for a measure currently being collected, or will that require new action?

- What existing data collection can be discontinued?[11]

Once the measures for the balanced scorecard have been finalized and definitions of each measure agreed upon, it should be possible for the library to prepare a summary that will clearly show the links between strategy and selected performance measures, as shown in Figure 10.6.

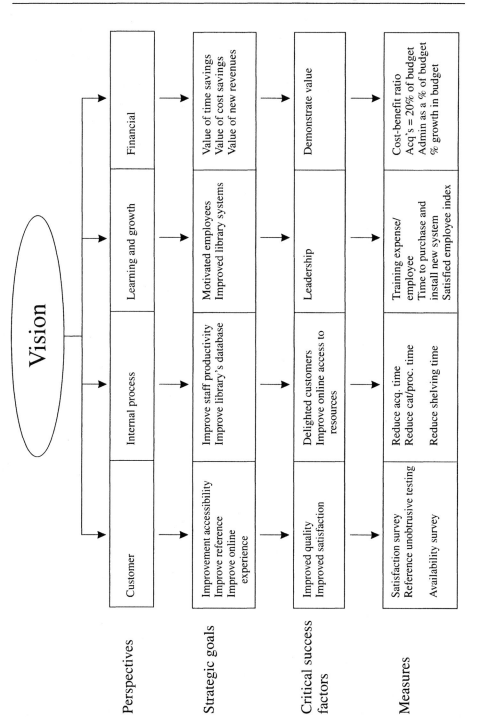

**Figure 10.6. Overview of Balanced Scorecard Development**

## Setting Goals

Once the performance measures have been determined for each perspective, it is important to establish a target or goal for each measure. The purpose of the goal is to make clear to all library staff members where the library should be using this particular measure. The target for each measure should be achievable over some period of time, for example, three years, but it should also be somewhat of a stretch. In addition to setting a target, the library should also set intermediate milestones, which may not be equidistant due to the cause-and-effect relationships between some perspectives.

Over the course of time, as a new scorecard is prepared, it will be possible to track the progress that is being made toward achieving the goal. In some cases, the progress is noted in a series of graphs that are shared with all staff members and other interested stakeholders. Part of the process of establishing a target or goal is to include time as an element for the target. For example, the library may wish to establish a 50 percent reduction in the gap between the current measure and the target measure, and this improvement should be achieved in "X" months.

## Initiatives

In some cases it may be necessary for the library to embark on a new program or initiative to improve a particular measure or set of measures. Such initiatives might include additional training for staff, investment in information technology, use of process reengineering, or benchmarking. Each initiative should have a clear "owner" so that the progress of the initiative or project can be tracked in parallel to noting the improvements on the scorecard itself.

# ACTION PLAN

Organizations that have successfully implemented scorecards have significantly altered traditional management practices to focus on strategy.[12] Rather than departmental, functional specialists, a strategy-focused organization will have cross-functional, integrated teams. Using the balanced scorecard allows the library to build management systems that revolve around strategies. A good test of a scorecard is to see if you can articulate the strategies of the library after reading only the balanced scorecard. If it appears that the scorecard reflects a collection of measures, then there probably is not a link with strategy.

The scorecard provides a framework, a language if you will, to communicate mission and strategy; it uses performance measures to inform library staff members about the drivers of current and future success. The hope is to channel the energies, the abilities, and the specific knowledge of library staff toward achieving the library's goals. The goal is to use the scorecard as the basis for planning rather than as a record-keeping activity. The real challenge is to ensure that all staff members add value to an organization on a continuous basis rather than periodically.

One of the major challenges facing any organization, including the larger library, is recognition that functional silos arise and become a barrier to strategy implementation. It can take time to remove the departmental barriers so that the library is focused on strategies. The goal is to move from programs and initiatives to focusing on improving the *outcomes* of the programs and initiatives. The small special library could participate with other units within its larger organization in developing a balanced scorecard for the larger organization as well as for the operating departments, including the library, within the organization.

One study found that managers and employees reacted positively to the measures found in a balanced scorecard and reorganized their resources and activities to improve their performance on these measures.[13] The study also found that subjective measures and one-way communication, that is, top-down, reduced the effectiveness of the balanced scorecard.

Once the measures that have been linked to the library' strategies have been identified for each perspective, the library needs to set targets or goals for improvement. After all, the whole purpose of the balanced scorecard is to measure how well the library is doing in terms of achieving its goals or targets. Measures are not the end; it's the improvement that is the end. Measures don't give an organization the answers but rather provoke a series of questions that should be raised. Once the questions have been answered, the library probably will identify process improvement activities that can be addressed. All this will happen when the results of the library balanced scorecard measurements are reported regularly to library staff, who can make changes and influence the measurements.

For example, a well-known study by Hernon and McClure resulted in the often-lamented and frequently cited 55 Percent Rule: Reference questions are answered completely and correctly about 55 percent of the time.[14] If 55 percent is not acceptable, what is? 90 percent? 70 percent? Does acceptable depend on the community served by the special library? Bourne has recommended that a library establish a 90 Percent Rule as a goal.[15]

The library should define an optimal, attainable goal for each measure and then periodically assess whether this goal is being reached. Clearly the attainment of the goal will not happen overnight, but the use of the balanced scorecard over time will establish the pattern of progress or stagnation that is actually being achieved. Depending on the time committed to developing a balanced scorecard, the elapsed time for developing the initial scorecard may be a few weeks in a small library and considerably longer for the larger library.

In summary, a library can move from a traditional organization using the budget as its primary controlling tool to a strategy-focused organization by doing the following:

- **Translating strategy into operational terms.** Use strategy maps to develop a library balanced scorecard.

- **Aligning the organization with the strategy.** Ensure that each department is aware of the strategies and the measures used to assess the strategies.

- **Making strategy known to everyone.** Make certain that all employees are aware of the change in operational performance measurement and that staff have a clear understanding of the balanced scorecard.

- **Making strategy a continual process.** Link budgets to strategies. Make sure that the information technology infrastructure is going to support the library's strategies. Determine whether employees will need additional training to meet the service delivery goals of the library.

- **Mobilizing change through executive leadership.** Use the balanced scorecard as a tool to drive the setting of the agenda for management and departmental meetings.

- **Making sure that measures are strategically relevant.** Use of the scorecard helps the library to focus on a limited number of important measures rather than the plethora of measures that have been used in the past.[16]

# TRAPS TO AVOID

The balanced scorecard approach is not without hazards. Among its potential problems are the following:

- The system can become too complex, with too many discrete measures. Most people can only keep about seven things in their heads at any one point in time.[17] With too many measures, it becomes impossible for the library's managers and employees to know what to focus on. It is easy to simply forget the whole thing due to its complexity. It is better to focus on a few vital measures that can make a significant difference. The library may wish to consider whether it is still necessary to continue to collect "traditional" measures that are now not a part of the scorecard.

- The measures may be subjective rather than objective. If measures are subjective, it is possible for bias to occur and people realize that ratings are not under their control. Therefore, people may tend to disregard the measures.

- Specific quantifiable measures may miss the important but intangible nature of library services. The search for the "correct" performance measures may mean that the library will miss the subtle elements of providing quality library services.

- Without a clear understanding of the balanced scorecard and how it "works," staff working to improve the "score" of one measure might degrade the performance of one or more other measures. Staff need to understand the cause-and-effect relationship between the strategies that have been adopted and the measures being used in the scorecard.

There should be consistent progress in reducing the gap between current performance and the target performance. A lack of steady progress toward achieving the goals is a sign that too many metrics are being used, the wrong metrics are being used, or the organization is not committed to constant improvement.

In time research will emerge about the appropriateness and efficacy of a particular measure and its use in conjunction with a specific strategy. But that will take some time as libraries report their experiences in using the balanced scorecard. Until then, the use of a particular measure or set of measures will require the common sense and experienced judgment of the library's management team.

Two researchers were able to use correlation analysis to discover the strength of the relationships between strategies in each of the four scorecard perspectives. For example, they were able to demonstrate that increased employee training and use of innovative techniques led to shorter product development times, which, in turn, led to higher sales and increased market share.[18]

For small special libraries, it should be possible to construct a balanced scorecard in a matter of a few weeks given the demanding day-by-day responsibilities of a librarian. For larger libraries, it may take several months to ensure the active participation of all the appropriate library staff members.

The balanced scorecard approach is not something that is done once and then dropped. Rather, it is a program that will require some time, and certainly some fine-tuning, to ensure that the scorecard has the right combination of metrics. A number of vendors have developed software[19] that assists organizations in automating the collection of information for the metrics, although the information could be easily maintained using a spreadsheet or even the tried and true paper and pencil. The popularity of the balanced scorecard approach, since its inception in the early 1990s, is reflected in the fact that the Balanced Scorecard Technology Council has more than 10,000 members.[20]

However, use of the balanced scorecard is not going to be a panacea that will solve any library's problems. The management team of any special library must stay in tune with the needs of its customers and how well the library is meeting those needs. The scorecard can be an important tool that will link a number of measures to the strategy of the library. Furthermore, the library balanced scorecard can be a useful asset when communicating with the library's stakeholders, staff members, and customers about the value of the special library. A sample of metrics that might be used in a balanced scorecard is shown in Figure 10.7 (page 138).

Birch has suggested that effective performance measurement is guided by the following seven rules:

1. **Performance measurement must be value-based**. A value-based focus is a way to ensure that the organization is directed toward achieving a strategic plan that has measurable results.

2. **Performance measures must influence the achievement of strategic objectives**. Measures linked to strategic objectives means that the library will be less likely to be distracted by short-term projects.

| | Complete Organization | Research Library | Legal Library |
|---|---|---|---|
| **Financial Strength**<br>*Looking back* | • Market share<br>• Revenue growth<br>• Operating profits<br>• Return on equity<br>• Growth in margins | • Revenue from patents issued in last three years<br>• Cost savings<br>• Time savings<br>• Number of peer-reviewed articles published | • Cost savings<br>• Time savings<br>• Increase in revenue from library services |
| **Customer Focus**<br>*Looking from the outside in* | • Customer satisfaction<br>• Customer retention<br>• Quality of customer service<br>• Revenue from new products or services | • Customer satisfaction<br>• Increase number of customers served<br>• Customer ratings of library services | • Customer satisfaction<br>• Increase number of customers served<br>• Customer ratings of library services |
| **Internal Operating Efficiency**<br>*Looking from the inside out* | • Delivery time<br>• Process quality<br>• Error rates<br>• Supplier satisfaction<br>• Costs | • Time to acquire documents<br>• Tech services cycle time<br>• Increase accuracy of reference services | • Amount of online searching<br>• Time to acquire documents<br>• Tech services cycle |
| **Learning and Growth**<br>*Looking ahead* | • Employee skill level<br>• Employee satisfaction<br>• Amount of absenteeism<br>• Training availability | • Employee turnover rate<br>• Number of grants received<br>• Training hours per staff | • Employee turnover rate<br>• Training hours per staff<br>• IT infrastructure |

Figure 10.7. Samples of Metrics Used in Balanced Scorecards

3. **Performance measures must not operate in a vacuum.** Performance measures that are linked to strategies and, in turn, strategies that are linked to the vision and values of the organization, will mean that all staff members will have a clear sense of what they need to do.

4. **Performance measures must not be sold as a self-contained solution.** Performance measures are a tool to assist a library in improving client satisfaction, effectiveness, and efficiency. But any set of measures will not bring change to a library. Rather, the measures can assist the library management team as they use their judgment and professional experience in moving the library to become an important part in the life of the larger organization.

5. **Rewards must be linked to performance.** Rewarding all staff members as the library moves closer to achieving its goals is an important way to demonstrate to staff the value of the balanced scorecard approach. People respond to the measures that are used to assess their performance.

6. **Performance measures must be comparable.** The library should be able to compare itself to other libraries to determine whether its goals are behind, in line with, or ahead of other similar libraries.

7. **Performance measures must provide a balanced view.** A balanced set of measures, especially measures that are linked to achieving specific strategies, will allow a library to see beyond its traditional boundaries and have a greater impact on the larger organization.[21]

# NOW WHAT?

A library interested in a systematic program of evaluation should have a clear understanding of the costs associated with providing a specific library service. This information can be obtained by using the ABC approach to identify all of the costs associated with the service or activity.

With an understanding of the costs of library services in place, the library should then solicit the participation of its customers in a needs assessment using, for example, a PAPE survey. A PAPE survey will tell the library what existing or planned services its customers deem most important and how well the library is currently doing in providing those services. The results of the survey allow the library to plan its processes and services so that they are based on the needs of its customers rather than the perceptions of library staff. A part of the PAPE survey can also ask the library's customers to identify what irritates them about the library.

Next the library should develop its own balanced scorecard that reflects its strategies for meeting the needs of customers and demonstrating real value to the parent organization. Larger special libraries may wish to develop a more narrowly defined set of measures for each department or area. These department-level balanced scorecards should be linked to the overall set of measures that the library has adopted for its balanced scorecard.

Clearly no one single measure will reflect the value and contribution of the library to the community. Librarians can quit searching for the one "perfect" measure and instead present a series of "good" measures using the format of the library balanced scorecard as the means to facilitate the communication process. An overview of a library balanced scorecard is shown in Figure 10.8.

## Customer Perspective

*Mission:*
Deliver value-adding products and services to end users

*Key question:*
Are the products and services provided by the library fulfilling the needs of the user community?

*Objectives:*
Satisfy customer information needs perceived as providing a responsive service Obtain materials in a timely manner

## Financial Perspective

*Mission:*
Contribute to the value of the organization

*Key question:*
Is the library accomplishing its goals and contributing value to the organization as a whole?

*Objectives:*
Ensure that library services provide Be business value
Communicate the value of the library to top management

## Internal Process Perspective

*Mission:*
Deliver library products and services in an efficient manner

*Key question:*
Does the library create, maintain, and deliver its products and services in an efficient manner?

*Objectives:*
Be efficient in planning and delivering library services
Be efficient in acquiring and maintaining the library's collection
Understand the costs for providing each library service

## Innovation and Learning Perspective

*Mission:*
Deliver continuous improvement and prepare for future challenges

*Key question:*
Is the library improving its products and services and preparing for potential changes and challenges?

*Objectives:*
Continuously upgrade staff skills through training and development
Regularly upgrade IT hardware and software

**Figure 10.8. Four Perspectives in a Library Balanced Scorecard**

# SUMMARY

The process of identifying the appropriate set of measures that will become the library's balanced scorecard will take some time to complete. Employing the recommended approach (using the mission statement to drive the selection of strategies, which determines the choice of measures) allows the library to link its strategies to a set of performance measures. These measures will have a cause-and-effect relationship to one another and to the ultimate goal of being linked to the library's strategies. Once developed, the library balanced scorecard can be used to assess the progress that is being made toward achieving the goals.

The balanced scorecard is a way for the library director to articulate and communicate the strategies of the library, which will help align individual and cross-departmental initiatives to achieve a common goal.

# NOTES

1. Rebecca Jones. Business Plans: Roadmaps for Growth & Success. *Information Outlook*, 4 (12), December 2000, 22–29.

2. Nils-Goran Olve, Jan Roy, and Magnus Wetter. *Performance Drivers: A Practical Guide to Using the Balanced Scorecard*. New York: John Wiley, 1999.

3. R. Charan and G. Colvin. Why CEOs Fail. *Fortune*, 139, June 21, 1999, 68–78. A similar analysis performed in the early 1980s noted the same result. See Walter Kiechel. Corporate Strategists Under Fire. *Fortune*, 106, December 27, 1982, 34–39.

4. Michael Porter. What Is Strategy? *Harvard Business Review*, November/December 1996, 61–79.

5. Gordon R. Sullivan. Quoted in Arthur Schneiderman. Why Balanced Scorecards Fail. *Journal of Strategic Performance Measurement* (Special Edition), January 1999, 7.

6. Mark Graham Brown. *Winning Score: How to Design and Implement Organizational Scorecards*. Portland, OR: Productivity, 2000.

7. S. Buchanan and F. Gibb. The Information Audit: An Integrated Approach. *International Journal of Information Management*, 18 (1), 1998, 29–47; D. Ellis, S. Barker, S. Potter, and C. Pridegon. Information Audits, Communication Audits and Information Mapping: A Review and Survey. *International Journal of Information Management*, 13 (2), 1993, 134–51.

8. Robert Kaplan and David Norton. The Balanced Scorecard: Measures That Drive Performance. *Harvard Business Review*, January/February 1992, 71–79.

9. Heinz Ahn. Applying the Balanced Scorecard Concept: An Experience Report. *Long Range Planning*, 34, 2001, 441–61.

10. David P. Norton. *Building a Management System to Implement Your Strategy. Point of View*. Lincoln, MA: Renaissance Solutions, 1996.

11. Richard L. Lynch and Kelvin F. Cross. *Measure Up! Yardsticks for Continuous Improvement*. London: Basil Blackwell, 1991.

12. Robert S. Kaplan. Strategic Performance Management and Management in Nonprofit Organizations. *Nonprofit Management & Leadership*, 11 (3), Spring 2001, 353–70.

13. Mary A. Malina and Frank H. Selto. *Communicating and Controlling Strategy: An Empirical Study of the Effectiveness of the Balanced Scorecard*. Available at http://www.BetterManagement.com (accessed July9, 2002).

14. Peter Hernon and Charles R. McClure. Unobtrusive Reference Testing: The 55 Percent Rule. *Library Journal*, 111 (8), April 15, 1986, 37–41.

15. Charles P. Bourne. Some User Requirements Stated Quantitatively in Terms of the 90 Percent Library, in Allen Kent and Orrin E. Taulbee (Eds.). *Electronic Information Handling*. Washington, DC: Spartan, 1965, 93–110.

16. Robert S. Kaplan and David P. Norton. *The Strategy-Focused Organization: How Balanced Scorecard Companies Thrive in the New Business Environment*. Boston: Harvard Business School Press, 2001.

17. G. A. Miller. The Magical Number Seven, Plus or Minus Two: Some Limits on Our Capacity for Processing Information. *Psychological Review*, 63, 1956, 81–97.

18. Khim Ling Sim and Hiam Chye Koh. Balanced Scorecard: A Rising Trend in Strategic Performance Measurement. *Measuring Business Excellence,* 5 (2), 2001, 18–26.

19. Balanced scorecard software has been developed by such large firms as PeopleSoft, SAP, and SAS as part of their suite of software products. Other providers of balanced software are Panorama Business Views, Pilot Software, CorVu Corporation, Gentia Software, Hyperion Solutions Corporation, and Soft Bicycle Company.

20. Visit the Balanced Scorecard Technology Council Web site at http://www.balancedscorecard.com.

21. Charles Birch. *Future Success: A Balanced Approach to Measuring and Improving Success in Your Organization.* New York: Prentice Hall, 2000.

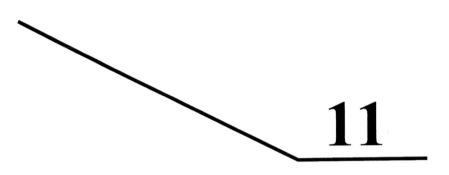

# 11

# Communicating the Value
# of a Special Library

*The very word "communicate" means "share," and
inasmuch as you and I are communicating at this moment,
we are one. No so much a union as a unity.*

—Colin Cherry

If a library puts together a plan to systematically gather performance data about the library and its information services, it will then need to communicate the results of these measures to its funding and administrative decision makers. The bottom line message, from a dollars-and-cents perspective, is that the library or information center generates revenue and saves more money than it costs.

Once you have the information about the impact of your library on the organization, "Toot your own horn!" Communicate a consistent message that information obtained from the library is valuable throughout your organization in a variety of ways. Susan DiMattia, former president of the Special Libraries Association, has suggested that librarians can share their value using the "7 Cs":

Competencies

Communication

Creativity

Correlation

Culture

Cheering

Chutzpah.[1]

# COMMUNICATION

Once the library has collected the performance measures needed to communicate to its larger organization or community, it should prepare a marketing plan so that the important message about the real value of the library can be communicated in a variety of ways to a range of stakeholders. The marketing plan should include both written materials and oral presentations.

Among the things that librarians need to keep in mind as they strive to convince management that library service is valuable are the following:

- Given the limited attention that people can pay to a plethora of messages, make sure that the message and the medium are matched appropriately.

- Be prepared! Know and rehearse your message so that when an opportunity presents itself, you can deliver the message about how your library provides value.

- Cultivate management of the larger organization, even when you don't need anything. Talk to management one-on-one whenever possible.

- Don't oversell your library services: *over-deliver.* Look for ways to establish relationships with your clients so that the librarian moves from being an information resource to a *partner* in solving problems with the client.[2]

- Educate but don't bore. Convey the message vividly but succinctly.

- Always maintain your credibility. Explain why the library and its information services are better equipped to meet the needs of its clients than other competing information services.

- Present information in terms that the audience will understand. Translate numbers, be they dollars or statistics, into terms that have a real associative meaning so that they will have greater impact and the bottom line message of the library will be heard, understood, and remembered. Often a graphic display of the information is easier to grasp rather than relying on text.

- Put information into a context. Rather than using dry statistics, provide some context that will be understandable in the environment within which the library operates. Use the language and perspective that your audience will normally use. Use anecdotes to demonstrate that the library made a real difference for a library customer.

## Focus on Benefits

When communicating with decision makers, customers, and potential users of the library, focus on benefits that result from use of the special library. Among the more important benefits are

- **Better decisions.** Typically, information provided by the library will help executives avoid making a poor decision.

- **Help in making decisions.** Information provided by the special library helps managers and executives choose an appropriate course of action.

- **Better work.** Library-provided information results in improved work.

- **Timely completion of work.** Information provided by the library helps employees complete their assigned tasks or activities faster.

- **Productivity increases.** Having the library acquire needed information allows employees to focus on getting their jobs done rather than looking for information.

- **Recognized achievement.** Those who are recognized within an organization as making significant contributions are more likely to be users of the special library.

- **Time savings.** Using library supplied-information allows an individual to avoid wasting the time of others when seeking an answer to a question. Information from the library will, in some cases, allow the individual to suggest changes in procedures or a process that will save the organization time.

- **Money savings.** In some cases, information from the library will result in changes that will save money for the organization through the adoption of best practices or a change in a process.

- **Generation of new revenue.** Information from the library may result in new product or service offerings, which attract new customers or increase revenues from existing customers.

## Written Materials

Prepare a written report documenting the results of your library's efforts to measure the value of the library and its information services. Librarians at the U.S. Department of Transportation prepared a wonderful report summarizing the value of information and it can be used as one model for a written report.[3] Distribute the executive summary of your report to all of your clients.

As well as preparing written materials, try the following:

- Create a Web site that posts the balanced scorecard and its associated measures so that all can see the progress that the library is achieving in terms of meetings its goals.

- Send out e-mail messages as a reminder of the library's commitment to using the balanced scorecard.

- Print a story about the value of the library and its information services in your larger organization's internal newsletter or intranet.

- Submit an article to one of the professional library journals documenting your experiences and results.

- Create an attractive annual report for the library. It doesn't have to be long, but it should offer substance about the ways in which your library provides value. What are the economic impacts, the cost-benefit ratio, or the ROI of the library on the larger organization?

- Use bookmarks as a way to get your message out.

In short, be creative!

## Oral Presentations

The library can prepare a number of oral presentations that range from the formal (using PowerPoint slides and handouts)[4] to the very informal, brief meetings that occur in hallways or elevators. A good salesperson is always practicing an "elevator speech," which is a brief (typically about 15 to 20 seconds) "executive summary" version of the "value" message. Library staff members should practice their elevator speeches about the value of the library.

Consistently use "war stories." Storytelling puts information in context and is a way to make facts and figures come alive. A good story is often the best way to convey the message about the value of the library and its information services. Stories have a human voice and help us to understand better.

## SUMMARY

Ultimately the measurement of performance in a special library is simple. If the library is not making a contribution to the overall performance of the company or organization, then the library will not survive. The library must be an essential part of any organization and make a contribution to the bottom line (however the bottom line is measured).

# NOTES

1. Susan DiMattia. To Endings and New Beginnings. *Information Outlook*, 4 (5), May 2000, 5.

2. Kevin Davis. The Changing Role of the Business Librarian. *Knowledge Management*, December 1998. Available at http://enterprise.supersites.net/knmagn2/km199812/fc1.htm (accessed July 9, 2002).

3. Susan C. Dresley and Annalynn Lacombe. *Value of Information and Information Services*. FHWA-SA-99-038. Washington, DC: Department of Transportation, October 1998.

4. Sally Gardner Reed. *Making the Case for Your Library: A How-to-Do-It Manual*. Number 104. New York: Neal-Schuman, 2001.

---

## The Bottom Line
### Information Obtained from Special Libraries Is Valuable

# Recommended Reading

## BOOKS

Birch, Charles. *Future Success: A Balanced Approach to Measuring and Improving Success in Your Organization.* New York: Prentice-Hall, 2000.

Brown, Mark Graham. *Winning Score: How to Design and Implement Organizational Scorecards.* Portland: Productivity, 2000.

Chang, Richard Y., and Mark W. Morgan. *Performance Scorecards: Measuring the Right Things in the Real World.* San Francisco: Jossey-Bass, 2001.

Kaplan, Robert S., and David P. Norton. *Translating Strategy Into Action: The Balanced Scorecard.* Boston: Harvard Business School Press, 1997.

————. *The Strategy-Focused Organization: How Balanced Scorecard Companies Thrive in the New Business Environment.* Boston: Harvard Business School Press, 2001.

Newcomer, Kathryn E. (Ed.). *Using Performance Measurement to Improve Public and Nonprofit Programs.* San Francisco: Jossey-Bass, 1997.

Olve, Nils-Gören, Jan Roy, and Magnus Wetter. *Performance Drivers.* New York: John Wiley, 1999.

## Articles

Chow, Chee W., Kamal M. Haddad, and James E. Williamson. Applying the Balanced Scorecard to Small Companies. *Management Accounting,* August 1997, 21–27.

Epstein, Mark J., and Jean-Francois Manzoni. The Balanced Scorecard and Tableau De Bord: Translating Strategy into Action. *Management Accounting,* August 1997, 28.

Gaiss, Michael. Enterprise Performance Management. *Management Accounting,* December 1998, p. 44.

Kaplan, Robert S. Devising a Balanced Scorecard Matched to Business Strategy. *Planning Review,* September–October 1994, 15.

Kaplan, Robert S., and David P. Norton. The Balanced Scorecard—Measures That Drive Performance, *Harvard Business Review,* January–February 1992, 71.

———. Linking the Balanced Scorecard to Strategy. *California Management Review*, Fall 1996, 53–79.

———. Putting the Balanced Scorecard to Work. *Harvard Business Review*, September–October 1993, 134.

———. Using the Balanced Scorecard As a Strategic Management System. *Harvard Business Review*, January–February 1996, 75.

———. Why Does Business Need a Balanced Scorecard. *Journal of Cost Management*, 11 (3), May/June 1997, 24–31.

———. Why Does Business Need a Balanced Scorecard (Part 1). *Journal of Strategic Performance Measurement*, 1 (1), February/March 1997, 5.

———. Why Does Business Need A Balanced Scorecard (Part 2). *Journal of Strategic Performance Measurement*, 1 (3), June/July 1997, 5.

Lingle, John H., and William A. Schiemannn. From Balanced Scorecard to Strategy Gauges: Is Measurement Worth It? *Management Review*, 85 (3), March 1996, 56–61.

Maisel, Larry. Performance Measurement: The Balanced Scorecard Approach. *Journal Of Cost Management*, 6 (2), Summer 1992, 47.

Poll, Roswitha. Performance, Processes and Costs: Managing Service Quality with the Balanced Scorecard. *Library Trends*, 49 (4), Spring 2001, 709–17.

Porter, Michael E. What Is Strategy? *Harvard Business Review*, November–December 1996, 61.

Schneiderman, Arthur. Why Balanced Scorecards Fail. *Journal of Strategic Performance Measurement*, Special Edition, January 1999, 6–11.

# Glossary

**Accelerated depreciation**. A method of depreciation that assigns more depreciation costs to the earlier years of an item's life and less to later years.

**Accumulated depreciation**. The total depreciation that has already been charged against the cost of an item.

**Activity based costing**. An accounting tool used to calculate realistic cost assignments based on actual resources consumed rather than arbitrary spreading according to formulas.

**Alignment**. Use of performance metrics in each area of an organization that are derived from a common strategic base and serve to align work efforts.

**Audit**. A planned and documented activity performed to determine the adequacy of and compliance with established procedures and instructions and the effectiveness of implementation.

**Balanced scorecard**. A management instrument that translates an organization's mission and strategy into a comprehensive set of performance measures and provides a framework for strategic measurement and management.

**Basis of allocation**. A measure of activity used to charge service department costs to other departments.

**Benchmark**. A standard or point of reference for measurement. Benchmarks that provide a range or averages allow an organization to compare performance in certain areas with other organizations.

**Benchmarking**. A systematic process for measuring products, services, and practices against external partners to achieve performance improvements.

**Best practices**. The best internal and external practices of an organization that produce superior performance

**Bibliometrics**. The application of statistical analysis to determine the publication patterns of books, journal articles, citations, and scholarly communications. Citation analysis is a major, but not the only, form of bibliometrics.

**Book value**. The value of a capital item on the accounting records, determined by subtracting accumulated depreciation from the original cost.

**Bradford distribution**. Named after S. C. Bradford, a British librarian and information scientist, who discovered a log normal, curve relationship among articles in a discipline and the journals publishing those articles; that is, a few journals publish the majority of articles.

**Business plan.** A plan developed to implement strategic goals and objectives at the business unit level of an organization.

**Capital budget.** A long-term plan for the acquisition, financing, and disposal of long-term assets.

**Charge back.** A process to recover costs from other departments within an organization through accounting charges to these departments. There is no actual exchange of money.

**Checklist method.** A traditional collection evaluation method that compares a list of bibliographical items against the holdings of a library.

**Core process.** The fundamental activities, or group of activities, so critical to an organization's success that failure to perform the process in an exemplary manner will result in deterioration of the mission.

**Cost accounting.** An accounting technique used to develop performance measures for operational control.

**Cost allocation.** The process of collecting and distributing costs.

**Cost-benefit analysis.** The comparison of the costs of an alternative with its associated benefits.

**Critical success factor.** A term popularized by John Rockart of MIT; it includes those few critical areas where things must go right for the business or organization to flourish.

**Customer satisfaction.** How customer expectations regarding quality and the delivery of library services compares to what is actually experienced.

**Cycle time.** The interval of time from the beginning to the end of a defined process. Receipt of order, cataloging and processing time, and return to shelf from circulation are examples of cycle time.

**Data.** The raw material of information (information provides meaning to the data). Typically data are numbers or text.

**Depreciation.** The accounting method used to spread the cost of an item over its useful life.

**Direct costs.** The costs directly traceable to the production of a particular product or service. These costs include the costs of materials and the costs of labor, such as salaries and benefits.

**Environmental scan.** A method used to identify external and internal factors that may potentially affect the organization.

**Fixed assets.** Assets that are expected to last for more than one year.

**Fixed costs.** Costs that do not change as the level of activity changes.

**Fringe benefit rate.** An average rate for fringe benefits throughout an organization, calculated by dividing total fringe benefit costs by total salary costs.

**Full cost.** The total cost of a product or service, including both direct and indirect costs.

**Goal.** A statement of the desired result to be achieved in a specified time. Goals are clear targets for specific action, are more detailed, and have shorter timeframes than objectives. A single objective may have multiple goals.

**Index.** Mathematically combines the results of several measures into a single composite measure.

**Indirect cost rate.** The total indirect costs of an organization divided by the total direct costs.

**Indirect costs.** Costs not directly associated with the manufacturing of a product or carrying out of a specific service. Examples include rent, utilities, and general administration. Sometimes called overhead.

**Information.** Information is data that have relevance, purpose, and meaning. Data become information when value is added by placing them in a context or providing structure.

**Information resource management (IRM).** Concerned with information assets, the content of information within the organization, and the people that handle the information

**Informed wealth.** The data, information, and knowledge in an organization.

**Intangible asset.** Nonphysical property of an organization, including research and development, patents and other intellectual property, training and development, brand names, and internally developed software.

**Key performance indicators.** Measurable factors of extreme importance to the organization in achieving the strategic goals, objectives, vision, and values, which if not implemented properly would likely result in significant decrease in customer satisfaction, employee morale, and financial management.

**Knowledge.** Arises from information combined with the experience, values, context, and expertise of an organization's employees. Knowledge can be embedded in documents but also is found in routines, processes, practices, and norms.

**Knowledge brokers.** Individuals within an organization, particularly librarians, who help connect those who need information and knowledge with those who have it.

**Knowledge value-added.** A methodology for determining for each process of an organization the amount of knowledge embedded in each subprocess that contributes to the overall process.

**Lag (lagging) indicator.** A measure that quantifies some characteristic after an event.

**Lead (leading) indicator**. A measure with proven predictive ability with respect to some outcome.

**Likert scale**. Used to indicate the extent to which a respondent agrees or disagrees with a statement or question.

**Measure**. One of several measurable values that contribute to the understanding and quantification of a key performance indicator.

**Measurement error**. The amount by which a measured result differs from its "true" value due to random variation or the design of the measurement process.

**Metrics**. The elements of a measurable system consisting of key performance indicators, measures, and measurement methodologies. Means the same as measurement.

**Moore's Law**. States that an information retrieval system will tend not to be used whenever it is more painful and troublesome for a customer to have information than for him or her not to have it.

**Neville's First Law of Serendipity**. States that to find anything one must be looking for something.

**Objective**. The general end toward which an organization directs its efforts. It is what an organization aims to accomplish. Objectives are also know as critical success factors.

**Opportunity cost**. The value gained or lost when a business decision is made to choose one alternative over others. The opportunity cost is calculated by comparing the net income associated with each alternative.

**Outcome**. The way customers respond to products or services.

**Output**. The products or services produced by a process.

**Overhead**. See Indirect costs.

**Payback period**. The time required for the savings or revenues from a project to accumulate to the amount of the initial investment.

**Performance measurement**. Feedback on activities that motivate behavior leading to continuous improvement in productivity, customer satisfaction, and so forth. It is not an employee evaluation.

**Performance measures**. Indicators of an organization's actions in achieving a given objective or goal. Such measures are generally divided into financial and nonfinancial.

**Present value**. The sum of money which, if invested now at a given rate of compound interest, will accumulate exactly to a specified amount at a specified future date.

**Pricing**. Establishing a monetary value for a service or product so that a customer can be charged. An indirect measure of value.

**Priority and performance evaluation (PAPE).** A survey methodology that asks the client to indicate the priority an organization or department should give to each service using a Likert scale. Following this, the client is asked to rate the perceived performance in providing the service.

**Process.** A group of sequenced work activities with a defined beginning and end.

**Process reengineering.** The fundamental rethinking and radical redesign of processes to bring about dramatic improvements. These process improvements are reflected in such performance measures as cost, quality, service, and speed.

**Quality.** Consistent conformity to customer expectations through the delivery of a product or service.

**Return on investment (ROI).** Typically, the ratio of net profits to total assets. For a project, it is the expected revenues divided by the anticipated costs.

**Semivariable cost.** A cost with both a fixed and a variable component. Sometimes called a semifixed cost.

**Shelf availability test.** A measure of how frequently patrons can immediately find the material they are seeking.

**Stakeholders.** Those who provide administrative and financial oversight to the operation of the library. Might include a library board, city council, or county board of supervisors. In some cases, stakeholders are meant to refer to other groups, for example library employees, library patrons, and library suppliers.

**Straight-line depreciation.** An accounting method for distributing the cost of an item evenly over its useful life.

**Strategic objectives.** Actions or changes required in the organization stated in measurable terms.

**Strategic planning.** The continuous and systematic process whereby guiding members of an organization make decisions about its future, develop the necessary procedures and operations to achieve that future, and determine how success is to be measured.

**Strategy.** Methods to achieve an organization's goals and objectives. Usually strategy is a planned approach to gain advantage and indicates how the organization will prevail over obstacles and its competition.

**Time value of money.** An economic theory that assumes that money is worth more today than at some point in the future.

**Trueswell's 80/20 Rule.** A bibliometric pattern, first observed by Richard Trueswell in 1969, that approximately 20 percent of a library's holdings account for 80 percent of its circulation.

**Validity**. The property of actually measuring what something is supposed to measure.

**Value**. Estimated or appraised worth; valuation.

**Value estimating**. Process of determining the value of information transactions for an organization .

**Value of information**. The worth, utility, or desirability that is assumed about information, demonstrated by it, or bestowed upon it, regardless of whether it is considered a commodity or a resource.

**Variable cost**. A cost that changes in direct proportion to changes in activity.

**Vision**. An idealized view of a desirable and potentially achievable future state; where or what an organization would like to be in the future.

# Appendix A

## Input Measures

| Measure | Definition |
|---|---|
| *Measure* | *Definition* |
| **Clients (Users):** | |
| Number of professionals in the organization | Count of the number of professionals in the organization. For example, lawyers, doctors, researchers, consultants, and so forth. |
| Registered clients per capita | Count of the number of registered clients divided by the total population of professionals |
| Total active registered users (used the library in the last two years) | Count of the number of registered users who have used the library in the last two years. Use include borrowing of materials, use of reference services, browsing the collection and so forth |
| | |
| **Budget:** | |
| Total budget of the library | Total budget allocation, in dollars |
| Total library budget as a percent of the organization's total budget | |
| Budget expenditures per professional staff member in the organization | Total budget allocation divided by the number of professional staff members in the larger organization |
| Budget expenditures for acquisitions | Proportion of budget spent on acquiring materials for the library's collection, expressed as a percentage |
| Materials acquisitions budget as a percent of the total budget | Proportion of budget spent on acquiring materials for the library's collection, expressed as a percentage |
| Acquisitions expenditure per item added | Expenditures spent on acquiring materials for the library's collection annually divided by the number of items added to the collection annually |

| Measure | Definition |
|---|---|
| Budget expenditures for periodicals | Proportion of budget spent on periodical (both print and electronic) subscriptions |
| Budget expenditures on one category as a proportion of library expenditures spent on all materials | Proportion of budget spent on one category as a proportion of library expenditures spent on all materials, expressed as a percentage |
| Acquisitions budget expenditures per capita | Total acquisitions budget divided by the total potential population served |
| Budget expenditures per FTE library staff | Total budget allocation divided by the total library staff (FTE) |
| Percent of library materials less than five years old | Number of titles (volumes) purchased in the last five years divided by thee total number of titles (volumes) |
| Expenditure per item added | Budget spent on acquiring materials for the library's collection divided by the total number of items added |
| Expenditure on staff | Budget spent on paying library staff, usually expressed as a percent of the total library budget |
| Expenditure per loan | Total budget allocation divided by the total circulation |
| Capital expenditures | Budget amount devoted to capital expenditures |
| Telecommunications expenditures | Budget amount devoted to telecommunications |
| Computer expenditures | Budget amount devoted to computer-related expenditures |
| | |
| **Staff**: | |
| Number of professional librarians | Total number of librarians (full-time equivalent) |
| Number of para-professionals | Total number of para-professionals (full-time equivalent) |
| Total number of staff | Total number of staff, all classifications (full-time equivalent) |
| Number of clients served per librarian | Count of the number of clients served divided by the number of librarians (FTE) |

| *Measure* | *Definition* |
|---|---|
| Number of clients served per staff member | Count of the number of clients served divided by the number of staff members (FTE) |
| Number of staff per capita | Count of the total number of staff divided by the total population |
| | |
| **Collection**: | |
| Total number of titles owned | Count of the total number of titles in the collection |
| Total number of volumes owned | Count of the total number of volumes in the collection |
| Volumes (Items) on shelves per capita | Count of the total number of volumes in the collection divided by total population, expressed as XX volumes per person |
| Number of print journal subscriptions | Count of the total number of current print journal subscriptions |
| Number of electronic journal subscriptions | Count of the total number of electronic journal subscriptions |
| Total number of serial titles offered | Count of paper-based journal titles plus count of full-text electronic journals available |
| Total number of titles purchased | Count of the total number of titles added to the collection annually |
| Total number of volumes purchased | Count of the total number of volumes added to the collection annually |
| Total number of titles in the collection per head of population served | Count of the total number of titles in the collection divided by the population served |
| Percent growth of collection | Count of the total number of titles (volumes) added to the collection annually divided by the total number of titles (volumes) in the collection at the start of the year, expressed as a percentage |
| Collection exchanges | Count of the total number of titles exchanged with another library/vendor during the year |

| Measure | Definition |
| --- | --- |
| Titles on order | Count of the total number of titles ordered annually |
| Titles (volumes) added per year per capita | Count of the total number of titles ordered annually divided by the total population |
| Feet (meters) of shelving per capita | Linear count, in feet, of available shelving for the collection |
| | |
| **Internet Workstations:** | |
| Number of public access Internet workstations | Count of the number of library owned public access, Web browser-based workstations that connect to the Internet |
| Number of public access Internet workstations in proportion to the legal service area population, public library measure | Count of the number of library owned public access, Web browser-based workstations that connect to the Internet compared to the service area population. For example, one Internet workstation for every 2,500 service population. |
| Speed of Internet workstations | Effective maximum bandwidth of Internet access –dependent upon the speed of the Internet connection and the speed of the LAN within the library. For example, 56 Kbps, 1.5 Mbps, and so forth. |
| **Databases:** | |
| Number of online, full-text titles available by subscription | Count of the number of full-text titles available online by subscription |
| | |
| **Space:** | |
| Total library floor space | Total floor space expressed in square feet |
| Public services floor space | Total floor space dedicated for public use, expressed in square feet |
| Library area per capita | Total population divided by the total floor space, expressed in XX people per square foot |

| Measure | Definition |
|---|---|
| Number of seats in the library | Count of the number of seats (chairs) for clients to use in the library |
| Number of seats per capita | Total population divided by the count of the number of seats in the library |
| Number of service points | Count of the number of service points, for example, circulation desk, reference desk, information desk and so forth. |
| Total hours open per week | Count of the total hours open per week (include hours for the main library plus branch libraries) |
| Hours open per 100 population | Count of the total hours open annually divided by the total population (in hundreds) |
| Equipment per capita | Count of the number of pieces of equipment per capita (by type) |
| Number of computer workstations available | Count of the number of computer workstations available for use by clients |
| Number of computer workstations available per capita | Count of the number of computer workstations available divided by the total population, expressed as a percentage |
| Computer workstations available annually per capita | Count of the number of computer workstations available times the number of hours the library is open annually divided by the total population, expressed as a percentage |
| Programs for Pre-School Children | Count of the number of programs offered annually for pre-school age children |
| Programs for School-Age Children | Count of the number of programs offered annually for school-age children |
| Total programs for children | Count of the number of programs offered annually for pre-school and school-age children |
| Attendance at Pre-School Programs | Count of the number of children attending pre-school programs annually |

| Measure | Definition |
| --- | --- |
| Attendance at School-Age Programs | Count of the number of children attending school-age programs annually |
| Total attendance at children's programs | Count of the number of children attending pre-school and school-age programs annually |

# Process Measures

| Measure | Definition |
| --- | --- |
| **Efficiency**: | |
| Cost of acquiring materials | Cost of the material plus staff salaries plus overhead (fringe benefits) to acquire materials for the collection |
| Cost of cataloging materials | Staff salaries plus overhead (fringe benefits) to catalog materials for the collection (may be broken up into copy cataloging costs, original cataloging costs, and total cataloging costs) |
| Cost of processing materials | Cost of supplies plus staff salaries plus overhead (fringe benefits) to physically process materials for the collection |
| Cost of reference services | Staff salaries plus overhead (fringe benefits) to provide reference services |
| Cost of circulation services | Staff salaries plus overhead (fringe benefits) to provide circulation services |
| | |
| **Staff Productivity**: | |
| Speed of acquiring materials | Elapsed time, in days, from the time an order is placed until the materials are received by the library |
| Speed of cataloging materials | Elapsed time, in days, from the time materials are received by the library until the cataloging is complete |

| Measure | Definition |
|---|---|
| Speed of processing materials | Elapsed time, in days, from the time materials have their cataloging completed and the materials are placed on the shelf |
| Speed of re-shelving borrowed materials | Elapsed time, in days, from the time materials are returned from circulation until they are returned to the shelves |
| **Library Information System Activity**: | |
| System reliability | Total number of hours system is available for use divided by total number of hours system should have been operating, normally expressed as a percentage |
| System down time (complimentary statistic for System Reliability) | 100 percent minus system reliability |
| Availability of public computer workstations | Number of hours the public computer workstations are available for use divided by the total number of hours the library is open, expressed as a percentage |

# Output Measures

| Measure | Definition |
|---|---|
| **Clients (Users)** | |
| Visits per capita | Count of the total number of people who enter the library each year divided by the population served |
| Visits per hour | Count of the total number of people who enter the library each year divided by the total number of hours the library is open each year |
| **The Budget**: | |
| Expenditure per client (user) | Total budget divided by the total number of clients (users) |
| Expenditure per borrower | Total budget divided by the total number of clients (users) who borrow materials |

| Measure | Definition |
| --- | --- |
| Expenditure per circulation loan | Total budget divided by the total number of circulations (annually) |
| Expenditure per reference transaction | Total budget divided by the total number of reference transactions (annually) |
| Expenditure per open library hour | Total budget divided by the total number of hours the library is open annually |
| **The Collection:** | |
| Circulation | Number of items charged out annually. Includes initial charge outs and renewals. Includes items from the general collection and reserves. Circulation data is often broken down into type of materials loaned, subject categories, and so forth. |
| In-library materials use | Number of items used in the library but not charged out. |
| Total materials use | The sum of circulation and in-library materials use. |
| Circulation per capita | Total circulation divided by population served |
| In-library materials use per capita | Number of items used in the library but not charged out divided by population served |
| Total materials use per capita | The sum of circulation and in-library materials use divided by population served |
| Circulation per staff | Total circulation divided by total number of staff (FTE) |
| Circulation per public services staff | Total circulation divided by total number of public services staff (FTE) |
| Circulation per hour open | Total circulation divided by total number of hours the library is open |
| Loans per visit | Average number of items borrowed per client visit |
| Loans per registered client | Total circulation divided by total number of registered clients |

| Measure | Definition |
|---|---|
| Collection turnover—average circulation per volume | Total circulation divided by total number of volumes in the collection |
| Proportion of circulating collection on loan | Count of the number of volumes on loan divided by the total number of volumes in the collection, expressed as a percentage |
| Circulation of new monographs | Count of the number of titles borrowed at least once during the past year compared to the total number of titles added to the collection during the last year, expressed as a percentage |
| Proportion of collection borrowed | Count of the number of volumes borrowed at least once during the year divided by the total number of volumes in the circulating collection, expressed as a percentage |
| Proportion of collection unused | Count of the number of volumes not borrowed (borrowed + in-library use) during the year divided by the total number of volumes in the circulating collection, expressed as a percentage |
| Proportion of collection borrowed, by subject categories | Count of the number of volumes borrowed at least once during the year, sorted by subject categories, divided by the total number of volumes in the circulating collection, sorted by subject categories, expressed as a percentage |
| Materials availability—sometimes called Measurement of Availability | Proportion of materials sought by a library client at the time of their visit available for use (on the shelf). Typically expressed as a percent. |
| Materials owned by the library | The probability that the materials sought by a client are owned by the library |
| Citation information correct | The probability that the client will bring complete and/or accurate citation information |
| Clients' skill at the catalog | The probability that the client is able to locate an item in the library's catalog which is owned by the library |

| *Measure* | *Definition* |
|---|---|
| Material on-the-shelf<br>Sometimes called shelf occupancy rate | The probability that the item sought by the client is not checked out |
| Material on-shelf | The probability that the desired item is to be found at its correct location on the shelf |
| Client location skills | The likelihood that the client is able to locate the item located on the shelf |
| Requested materials delay | Time users must wait for the desired material — normally expressed in days |
| Amount of intra-system movement of materials | Count of the number of items moved from one (branch) library to another to fulfill the request of a client |
| Intra-system materials delay | Time users must wait for the desired material — normally expressed in days |
| Workload per staff member | Total circulation divided by total staff (FTE). It should be recognized that an item checked out (charged) must also later be checked back in (returned). |
| Overdues per circulation | Count of the number of items overdue divided by annual circulation |
| Turnaround time for shelving books | Count of the number of hours (days) it takes to return a borrowed item that has been returned to the library back to the shelf |
| **Technical Services**: | |
| Number of titles ordered | Count of the number of titles ordered |
| Number of purchase orders placed | Count of the number of purchase orders placed |
| Number of materials cataloged | Count of the number of items cataloged |
| Number of journal issues received | Count of the number of journal issues received |
| Number of journals routed | Count of the number of journal routed |
| | |

| Measure | Definition |
|---|---|
| **Reference Services**: | |
| Number of reference transactions | A reference transaction is an information contact that involves the knowledge, use, recommendation, interpretation, or instruction of one or more information resources between a library client and a library staff member. Typically directional questions are not counted. Libraries will sometimes sort by those transactions that take less than 10 minutes and those transactions that take more than 10 minutes. |
| Proportion of correctly answered reference transactions | "Test" reference questions are provided to volunteer clients. The clients ask the question and record several things about the reference process, including the answer. The provided answer is then compared to the "correct" answer and the percent correctly answered is calculated. |
| Number of virtual reference transactions | Annual count of the number of reference transactions received and responded to electronically, email, Web form, chat (and in the future, videoconferencing). |
| Reference transactions per circulation | Total number of annual reference transactions divided by total circulation |
| **Document Delivery**: | |
| Number of documents ordered | Count of the number of documents ordered |
| Document delivery fill rate | Proportion of the number of documents received compared to the number of documents ordered, expressed as a percentage |
| Speed of document delivery | Time from when a document order is placed until the document is received, expressed in number of days (hours) |

| *Measure* | *Definition* |
|---|---|
| Cost of document delivery | Total of the charges incurred to order documents using a document delivery service. Would include any annual minimum subscription charge plus the per transaction charges. |
| Turnaround time for photocopies | Time from when a photocopy request is placed until the photocopy is received by the client, expressed in number of days (hours) |
| **Interlibrary Loan (ILL):** | |
| Number of items requested | Count of the number of items requested from another library |
| ILL fill rate | Proportion of the number of items received compared to the number of items requested, expressed as a percentage |
| Speed of ILL | Time from when an item request is placed until the item is received, expressed in number of days (hours) |
| ILL fees | Fees charged by other libraries to loan a item to another library |
| Requests received form other libraries | Count of the number of requests received from another library |
| ILL requests as a proportion to total circulation | Count of the number of items requested from another library divided by total circulation |
| ILL photocopies | Number of photocopy pages produced to meet client ILL needs |
| | |
| **Information Alerting:** | |
| Number of current information alerts (sometimes called selective dissemination of information or SDI) | Count of the number of current information alerts sent to clients (alerts may be sent using email or snail mail) |
| Number of current information alert users | Count of the number of current information alert users |
| **Library Information System:** | |

| Measure | Definition |
|---|---|
| Number of staff hours spent servicing information technology in public service areas | Total number of staff hours (information technology staff, professional librarian, para-professional, clerical and volunteers) spent in service information technology in public service areas (typically data gathered during a one-week sample period). |
| **Online Catalog:** | |
| Number of online catalog search sessions | Count of the total number of user search sessions |
| Number of online catalog searches | Count of the number of online catalog searches, often sorted by types of searches. |
| Number of successful online catalog searches | Count of the number of online catalog searches that retrieve some records but retrieve fewer than some number (generally less than 100 records). |
| Number of items/records examined | Count of the number of full-text articles/ pages, abstracts, and citations viewed. In some cases, these statistics are sorted: text only and text/graphics viewed. |
| | |
| **Public Access Internet Workstations:** | |
| Number of public access Internet users | Count of the total number of users of all of the library's Internet workstations (typically the count is done using a one-week sample) |
| Average annual use of Internet workstations | Count of the number of hours the library owned Internet workstations are busy divided by (the number of library owned Internet workstations times the number of hours the library is open). Usually expressed as a percentage. |

| Measure | Definition |
|---|---|
| **Databases:** | |
| Number of database sessions | Total count of the number of sessions (logins) initiated to the online databases. Some libraries track sessions initiated from within the library, outside sessions and total sessions. |
| Number of database queries/searches | Count of the number of searches conducted in the online databases. Subsequently actions by the user, for example, sorting, printing, are not counted. |
| Number of items/records examined | Count of the number of full-text articles/ pages, abstracts, and citations viewed. In some cases, these statistics are sorted: text only and text/graphics viewed. |
| **Virtual Visits:** | |
| Number of virtual visits to networked library resources | Count of visits to the library via the Internet (and dial-in access, if provided). Visits to the library's Web site, the library's online catalog, and access to online databases. |
| **Facilities and Library Use:** | |
| Attendance | Number of user visits to the library |
| Remote uses | Number of library clients who visit the library's Web site and online catalog remotely. |
| Total uses of the library | The sum of attendance and remote uses. |
| Facilities use rate | Proportion of time, on average, that a facility is being used. All kinds of uses are included: user seating, workstations, photocopy machines, reference services, use of the collection and so forth. |
| Service point use | Average number of users at a public service point. For example, reference, circulation or information desks. |

| *Measure* | *Definition* |
|---|---|
| Building use | Average number of people in the library at any one time. |
| Use of library equipment | Count of the number of hour's library equipment is used. For example, microform machines, photocopiers and so forth. |
| Number of photocopies produced | Count of the number of photocopies produced |
| Seat occupancy rate | Count of the number of seats (chairs) being used compared to the total number of seats |
| **Instruction**: | |
| Client information technology instruction | Total number of clients instructed and total number of client instruction hours |
| Staff information technology instruction | Total number of staff instructed and total number of staff instruction hours |
| **Out-of-library services**: | |
| Number of persons served | Count of the number of persons served by the outreach programs. For example, delivering library materials to the home bound, senior citizen clubs, book deposits, and so forth |
| Bookmobile circulation | Count of the number of items loaned via the bookmobile |
| People served by the bookmobile | Count of the number of people who use the bookmobile service |
| Number of bookmobile stops | Count of the number of bookmobile stops |

# Appendix B

## Sample PAPE Survey

In your opinion, what priority should the library give each of the following?

Please circle the number that best gives an indication of your assessment.

| | Low Priority | | | | | Very High Priority | | Don't Know |
|---|---|---|---|---|---|---|---|---|
| | <——————————————————————————————> | | | | | | | |
| Availability and accessibility of library staff | 1 | 2 | 3 | 4 | 5 | 6 | 7 | D |
| Accuracy of information services | 1 | 2 | 3 | 4 | 5 | 6 | 7 | D |
| Timelines of information services | 1 | 2 | 3 | 4 | 5 | 6 | 7 | D |
| Information alert service | 1 | 2 | 3 | 4 | 5 | 6 | 7 | D |
| Document delivery service | 1 | 2 | 3 | 4 | 5 | 6 | 7 | D |
| Access to online databases | 1 | 2 | 3 | 4 | 5 | 6 | 7 | D |
| Books and journals delivered to my office | 1 | 2 | 3 | 4 | 5 | 6 | 7 | D |
| 24-hour response to reference questions delivered via telephone or e-mail | 1 | 2 | 3 | 4 | 5 | 6 | 7 | D |
| Photocopies of tables of contents from selected journals delivered to my office | 1 | 2 | 3 | 4 | 5 | 6 | 7 | D |
| Order materials for me | 1 | 2 | 3 | 4 | 5 | 6 | 7 | D |
| New books alert service | 1 | 2 | 3 | 4 | 5 | 6 | 7 | D |
| Online database searched for me | 1 | 2 | 3 | 4 | 5 | 6 | 7 | D |
| Quite space for reading and research | 1 | 2 | 3 | 4 | 5 | 6 | 7 | D |
| Ability to browse the library's collection | 1 | 2 | 3 | 4 | 5 | 6 | 7 | D |

|  | Low Priority | | | | | Very High Priority | | Don't Know |
|---|---|---|---|---|---|---|---|---|
| | <------------------------------------------------> | | | | | | | |
| Access to technical reports collection | 1 | 2 | 3 | 4 | 5 | 6 | 7 | D |
| Full-text accesss to the technical reports collection | 1 | 2 | 3 | 4 | 5 | 6 | 7 | D |
| Access to a collection of professional journals | 1 | 2 | 3 | 4 | 5 | 6 | 7 | D |

In your opinion, how well does the library perform in each of the following areas?

Please circle the number that best gives an indication of your assessment.

|  | Low Priority | | | | | Very High Priority | | Don't Know |
|---|---|---|---|---|---|---|---|---|
| | <------------------------------------------------> | | | | | | | |
| Access to a collection of professional jounals | 1 | 2 | 3 | 4 | 5 | 6 | 7 | D |
| New books alert service | 1 | 2 | 3 | 4 | 5 | 6 | 7 | D |
| Online databases searched for me | 1 | 2 | 3 | 4 | 5 | 6 | 7 | D |
| Ability to browse the library's collection | 1 | 2 | 3 | 4 | 5 | 6 | 7 | D |
| Full-text access to the technical reports collection | 1 | 2 | 3 | 4 | 5 | 6 | 7 | D |
| Quiet space for reading and research | 1 | 2 | 3 | 4 | 5 | 6 | 7 | D |
| Access to online databases | 1 | 2 | 3 | 4 | 5 | 6 | 7 | D |
| Availability and accessibility of library staff | 1 | 2 | 3 | 4 | 5 | 6 | 7 | D |
| Order materials for me | 1 | 2 | 3 | 4 | 5 | 6 | 7 | D |
| Accuracy of information services | 1 | 2 | 3 | 4 | 5 | 6 | 7 | D |
| Photocopies of tables of contents from selected journals delivered to my office | 1 | 2 | 3 | 4 | 5 | 6 | 7 | D |
| Timeliness of information services | 1 | 2 | 3 | 4 | 5 | 6 | 7 | D |

| | Low<br>Priority<br><———————————————————> | | | | Very High<br>Priority | | | Don't<br>Know |
|---|---|---|---|---|---|---|---|---|
| Books and journals delivered to my office | 1 | 2 | 3 | 4 | 5 | 6 | 7 | D |
| Information alert services | 1 | 2 | 3 | 4 | 5 | 6 | 7 | D |
| Access to technical reports collection | 1 | 2 | 3 | 4 | 5 | 6 | 7 | D |
| Document delivery service | 1 | 2 | 3 | 4 | 5 | 6 | 7 | D |
| 24-hour response to reference questions<br>delivered via telephone or e-mail | 1 | 2 | 3 | 4 | 5 | 6 | 7 | D |

Note: Obviously a library needs to add, edit, and delete the list of available and/or planned services to reflect its situation.

# Appendix C

## Library Benefits Survey

The purpose of this survey is to determine the impact that the Library or Information Center has had on your job in the last 12 months.

1. Did the library help you save time?    Y_____ N____

   If yes, considering the instances you used the Library, what percent saved you time?    _____%

   How much time did you save (in hours)?    _____ hours

2. Did the library help you generate new revenue?  Y_____ N____

   If yes, considering the instances you used the Library, what percent helped you generate new revenue?    _____%

   How much new revenue did you generate?  $_____

3. Did the library help you save money?    Y_____ N____

   If yes, considering the instances you used the Library, what percent helped you save money?    _____%

   How much money did you save?    $_____

4. Did the library cost you time?    Y_____ N____

   Obtaining information of little value.

   If yes, considering the instances you used the library, what percent cost you time?    _____%

   How much time did the information    _____ hours
   cost you (in hours)?

5. Did the library cost you money?    Y_____ N____

   Obtaining inaccurate information.

   If yes, considering the instances you used the Library, what percent cost you money?    _____%

   How much money did the information    $_____
   cost you?

# Return on Investment (ROI) Calculation

Time saved  x  Number of active customers  x  Average salary per hour

= Savings in time expressed as dollars

Revenue generated/dollars saved  x  Number of active customers

= Revenue generated/dollars saved

Less:

Time spent/wasted  x  Number of active customers

x  Average salary per hour  =  Loss in time expressed as dollars

Cost of inaccurate information  x  Number of active customers

= Cost of inaccurate information

Net benefits

Library budget

ROI  =  Net benefits  /  Library budget

# Index